THE BEST WALKS
IN **BRITAIN**

THE BEST WALKS
IN BRITAIN

p

This is a Parragon Book
This edition published in 2006

Parragon
Queen Street House
4 Queen Street
Bath BA1 1HE
United Kingdom

 This product includes mapping data
licensed from Ordnance Survey®
with the permission of the Controller of Her Majesty's
Stationery Office. © Crown copyright 2003.
All rights reserved. Licence number PU 100039050.

ISBN: 1–40544–369–3

Printed in Indonesia

www.walkingworld.com

Visit the Walkingworld website at
www.walkingworld.com

All the walks in this book are available in more
detailed form on the Walkingworld website.
The route instructions have photographs at key
decision points to help you to navigate, and
each walk comes with an Ordnance Survey®
map. Simply print them out on A4 paper
and you are ready to go! A modest annual
subscription gives you access to over 1,400
walks, all in this easy-to-follow format. If you
wish, you can purchase individual walks for a
small fee.

Next to every walk in this book you will see
a Walk ID. You can enter this ID number on
Walkingworld's 'Find a Walk' page and you will
be taken straight to the details of that walk.

CONTENTS

Introduction

Britain is a fabulous place to walk. We are blessed with a varied and beautiful landscape, a dense network of public footpaths and places of historical interest at every corner. Add to all this the many thousands of well-placed pubs, tea shops and visitor attractions, and it's easy to see why walking is a treasured pastime for millions of people.

Walking is the perfect way to keep fit and healthy. It is good for your heart, muscles and body generally, without making the extreme demands of many sports. For most walkers, however, the health benefits are secondary. We walk for the sheer pleasure of it – being able to breathe in the fresh air, enjoy the company of our friends and 'get away from it all'.

Equipment

If you take up walking as a hobby, it is quite possible to spend a fortune on specialist outdoor kit. But you really don't need to. Just invest in a few inexpensive basics and you'll be ready to enjoy any of the walks in this book.

For footwear, boots are definitely best as they provide you with ankle support and protection from the inevitable mud, nettles and puddles. A light-weight pair should be fine if you have no intention of venturing up big hills or over rugged terrain. If you are not sure what to get, go to a specialist shop and ask for advice. Above all, choose boots that fit well and are comfortable.

Take clothing to deal with any weather that you may encounter. Allow for the 'wind-chill' factor – if your clothes get wet you will feel this cooling effect even more. Carry a small rucksack with a spare top, a hat and waterproofs, just in case. The key is to be able to easily put on and take off layers of clothing at will and so keep an even, comfortable temperature throughout the day.

It's a good idea to carry some food and drink. Walking is exercise and you need to replace the fluid you lose through perspiration. Take a bottle of soft drink or water, and sip it regularly rather than downing it in one go. The occasional chocolate bar, sandwich or biscuit can work wonders when energy levels are flagging.

Walking poles – the modern version of the walking stick – are worth considering. They help you to balance and allow your arms to take some of the strain when going uphill. They also lessen the impact on your knees on downhill slopes. Don't be fooled into thinking that poles are just for the older walker – they are popular with trekkers and mountaineers of all ages.

Finding your way

Most walkers use Ordnance Survey® maps, rightly considered to be among the most accurate, up-to-date and 'walker–friendly' in the world. The 1:50,000 scale Landranger series has long been a favourite of outdoor enthusiasts. Almost all areas of Britain are also covered by the more detailed 1:25,000 scale Explorer and Explorer OL series. These include features such as field boundaries, farm buildings and small streams.

Having a map and compass – and learning how to use them – is vital to being safe in the countryside. Compass and map skills come with practice – there is no substitute for taking them out and having a go. Buy a compass with a transparent base plate and rotating dial; you will find this type in any outdoor shop. Most come with simple instructions – if not, ask in the shop for a guide.

If this all sounds a bit serious, I urge you not to worry too much about getting lost. We have all done it – some of us more often than we care to admit! You are unlikely to come to much harm unless you are on a featureless hilltop or out in very poor weather. If you want to build up your confidence, start with shorter routes through farmland or along the coastline and allow yourself plenty of time.

There are plenty of walks in this book that are perfect for the beginner. You can make navigating even easier by downloading the routes in this book from Walkingworld's website: www.walkingworld.com. These detailed walk instructions feature a photograph at each major decision point, to help you confirm your position and see where to go next. Another alternative is to join a local walking group and learn

key to maps

☏	Telephone	⛟	Lighthouse
◉	Start of route		Camping
	Viewpoint	▲	Youth hostel
⋀	Pylon		Bridge
	Triangulation point		Windmill
⋎	Radio mast		Highest point/summit
⌘	Church with Steeple	PH	Public house
+	Church without Steeple	PC	Public convenience
⚲	Chapel	1666	Place of historical interest
⋏	Power		Embankment/cutting
⚑	Golf course		Rocky area/ sharp drop
	Picnic area	▪	Building
	Car park	▨	Castle
	Information	☆	Tumulus
		⁙	Garden

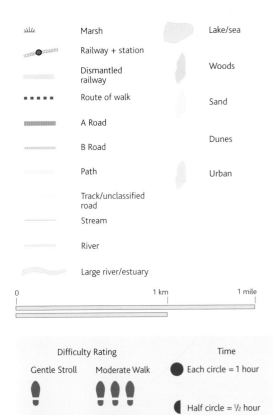

⁄⁄⁄	Marsh		Lake/sea
●━━	Railway + station		Woods
	Dismantled railway		
▪ ▪ ▪ ▪ ▪	Route of walk		Sand
	A Road		
	B Road		Dunes
	Path		Urban
	Track/unclassified road		
	Stream		
	River		
	Large river/estuary		

0   1 km   1 mile

Difficulty Rating   **Time**

Gentle Stroll   Moderate Walk   ● Each circle = 1 hour

Easy Walk   Hill Scramble   ◖ Half circle = ½ hour

from others. There are hundreds of such groups around the country, with members keen to share their experience and skills.

Enough words. Take the walks in this book as your inspiration. Grab your map and compass, and put on your boots. It's time to go out and walk!

Have fun.

DAVID STEWART *Walkingworld*

Scotland

Coastal & Waterside

Scotland's waterside walks take in wave-beaten crags, silent lochs and roaring waterfalls. Highlights include Dunskey Castle, Grey Mare's Tail, Herma Ness and Flowerdale Falls.

▲ Map: Explorer 309

▲ Distance: 9 km/5¼ miles

▲ Walk ID: 824 Tony Brotherton

Difficulty rating

Time

▲ Hills or Fells, Sea, Pub, Toilets, Church, Castle, Wildlife, Birds, Flowers, Great Views, Butterflies, Food Shop

Dunskey Castle from Portpatrick

From the port of Portpatrick this scenic walk heads south over the moorland byroad, passing by the ruin of Dunskey Castle with its dramatic cliff-top setting. The splendid coastal scenery, birds and flowers make this a walk to remember.

❶ From the car park pass by the old lighthouse and walk round the harbour as far as Main Street. Turn into Main Street, then into School Brae. Follow the road uphill and across the old railway bridge to the junction with the Old Military Road.

❷ Follow this road. It rises clear of Portpatrick and meets a junction. Keeping on the road, turn right across the moors to reach the old railway viaduct.

❸ Continue along this moorland road. At the stone wall, pause to view Dunskey Castle in the distance. The road switchbacks on, past a joining road at North Port O'Spittal, then drops and bends sharply before the turn-off to Knockinaam Lodge Hotel. Turn right down the lane towards the hotel.

❹ At the top of the hotel car park, a sign points the way to Portpatrick via a cliff walk. The path climbs to the right. At the top cross two fields, exiting via the gate at the top corner of the second field. The curving path to the left leads down to Morroch Bay.

❺ Follow the path along the top of the cliffs, crossing occasional stiles. Look out for abundant birdlife on rocks and cliff-ledges. Dunskey Castle comes into view again and the path descends to a bridge over the burn. Cross the bridge and ascend the steps. The path meanders over the headland to Castle Bay.

❻ Follow the path round the top of the bay to Dunskey Castle. The path continues along the cliff top, with the old railway cutting below to the right. Portpatrick Hotel comes into sight. Follow the steps down to Portpatrick harbour. To return to the car park, retrace your steps by the old lighthouse.

A beautiful view of Portpatrick harbour, seen from the cliffs to the north.

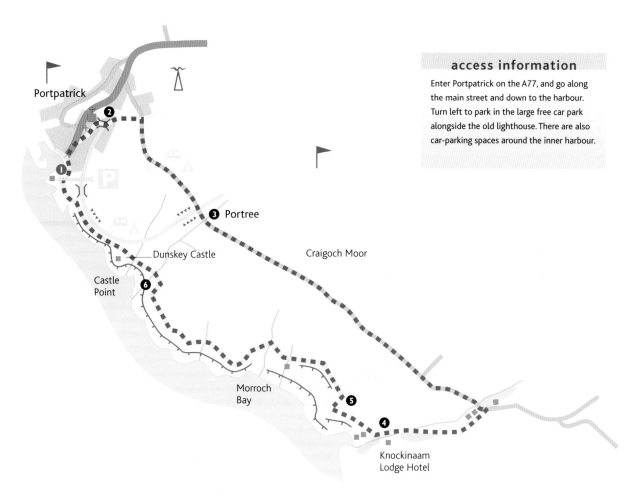

Portpatrick

2

1

3 Portree

Dunskey Castle

Castle
Point

6

Craigoch Moor

Morroch
Bay

5

4

Knockinaam
Lodge Hotel

access information

Enter Portpatrick on the A77, and go along the main street and down to the harbour. Turn left to park in the large free car park alongside the old lighthouse. There are also car-parking spaces around the inner harbour.

The ruins of Dunskey Castle stand out as a clear landmark at the top of the cliff.

further information

Look out for fulmars, kittiwakes, guillemots and peregrine falcons around the cliffs above Morroch Bay. Unusual wild flowers, including spring squill and orchids, grow among the more common thrift and campion.

0   1 km   1 mile

▲ Map: Explorer 330
▲ Distance: 11 km/6¾ miles
▲ Walk ID: 301 Simon Tweedie

Difficulty rating

!!!

Time

●●●●

▲ Hills or Fells, Mountains, River, Lake/Loch, National Trust/NTS, Wildlife, Birds, Flowers, Great Views

White Coomb from Grey Mare's Tail

This outstanding walk takes you to one of Scotland's highest waterfalls (known as the Grey Mare's Tail), a hidden glen and Loch Skeen. Listen out for the high-pitched call of the peregrine falcons which nest on the craigs.

❶ Leave by the steps on the north side of the car park. The path is steep and rises quickly to reveal spectacular views.

❷ When you reach the top of the falls, the glen above opens out. The path meanders, following the gentle flow of the burn. White Coomb looms high to the left with Lochcraig Head to the north. Continue on upwards until Loch Skeen comes into view to the left of the path.

❸ The route follows the eastern shore of the loch with no discernible path. Leaving the loch behind, the ground rises steeply. Follow a route to the east of the cliffs and up the steep grassy slope to the cairn at the top of Lochcraig Head. Follow the dry-stone dyke left towards White Coomb.

❹ At Firthybrig Head the dyke takes a sharp left to a southerly direction. Follow this through Donald's Cleuch Head to Firthhope Rig. Here the dyke takes a sharp left. Follow the dyke a short way until it bears left. This is the closest landmark to the summit cairn, which lies about 100 paces to the south west.

❺ Return to the dyke from the summit and follow it down the hill until you reach Rough Craigs. Scramble down to the left of the dyke until you pick it up again at the bottom. Follow the dyke over Upper Tarnberry and down to meet the Tail Burn.

❻ The dyke ends on the Tail Burn where you cross. Pick up the Tail Burn path again on the other side and follow it back down to the car park.

A stand of Scots Pine, seen from Moffat Water.

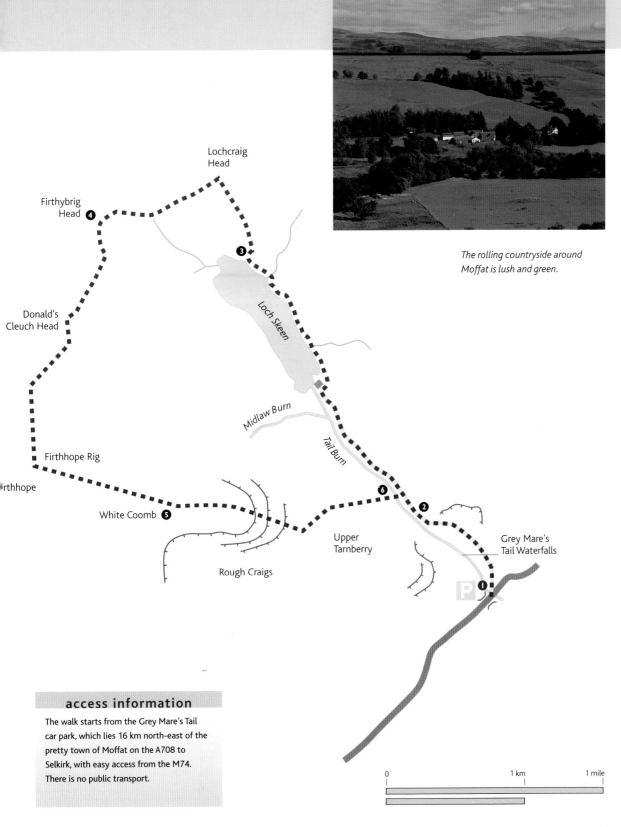

Lochcraig
Head

Firthybrig
Head ❹

❸

Donald's
Cleuch Head

Loch Skeen

Firthhope Rig

Firthhope

White Coomb ❺

Midlaw Burn

Tail Burn

❻

❷

Upper
Tarnberry

Rough Craigs

Grey Mare's
Tail Waterfalls

P ❶

*The rolling countryside around
Moffat is lush and green.*

access information

The walk starts from the Grey Mare's Tail
car park, which lies 16 km north-east of the
pretty town of Moffat on the A708 to
Selkirk, with easy access from the M74.
There is no public transport.

0   1 km   1 mile

▲ Map: Explorer 470

▲ Distance: 7 km/4¾ miles

▲ Walk ID: 1508 C. & J. Simpson

Difficulty rating

Time

▲ Sea, Birds, Flowers, Great Views, Moor, Nature Trail

Herma Ness

This walk is a superb mix of moorland and coastal walking to the cliffs of Herma Ness with its fine arches and array of offshore sea stacks. The return over Hermaness Hill gives good views over Muckle Flugga and its lighthouse.

❶ From the car park, go through the gate, uphill a few metres and through another gate to follow the path which traverses the hillside, rising gently as you go. In time this leads to and then follows the burn of Winnaswarta Dale.

❷ Shortly after you start following the burn you come to a fork and a marker post. Take the left-hand fork. (The return route comes in on the path on the right.) There follows a gradually rising section across open moor, with occasional stretches of boardwalk to protect sensitive areas of bog.

❸ At the marker post the view along the cliffs is spectacular, with thousands of seabirds. The route turns right and follows the cliffs, dipping slightly before rising again.

❹ As you start to rise again the views over to the rock arch, the stacks and Muckle Flugga lighthouse open out.

❺ For the return journey, marker posts leading off to the right take you up a well-worn path to the top of Hermaness Hill. The top of the hill has some lochans (small lakes) and more boardwalk sections. There are good views from the top of the hill although, in contrast to the wilderness on this side of the Burra Firth, Saxa Vord, the hill on the other side, is topped by a prominent early warning station. The descent over more boggy ground with numerous lochans is

marked by a series of posts leading back to the junction.

❻ Rejoin the outward route further down the burn. Go back along the path to the car park.

The jagged rocks off the coast of Herma Ness are the northernmost point of Britain, and home to thousands of seabirds.

access information

The island of Unst is reached by two ferries from the Shetland mainland, including a drive over the island of Yell in between. On Unst follow the main road through Baltasound towards Haroldswick. Take the unclassified road on your left as you approach Haroldswick – signposted to Herma Ness and Burrafirth.

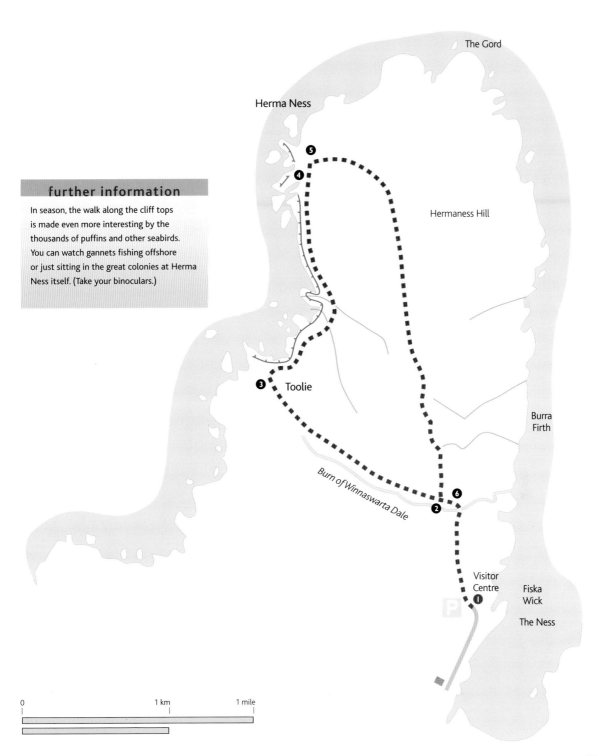

The Gord

Herma Ness

Hermaness Hill

further information

In season, the walk along the cliff tops
is made even more interesting by the
thousands of puffins and other seabirds.
You can watch gannets fishing offshore
or just sitting in the great colonies at Herma
Ness itself. (Take your binoculars.)

Toolie

Burra
Firth

Burn of Winnaswarta Dale

Visitor
Centre

Fiska
Wick

The Ness

0   1 km   1 mile

▲ Map: Explorer 416

▲ Distance: 4 km/2½ miles

▲ Walk ID: 794 D. B. Grant

Difficulty rating

👣👣

Time

◖●◖

▲ River, Lake/Loch, Pub, Toilets, Birds, Flowers, Great Views, Public Transport, Nature Trail, Waterfall, Woodland

Falls of Foyers.

The Falls of Foyers

This is a short walk to enjoy at Foyers on the south shore of Loch Ness. Foyers is in two parts, Upper and Lower. The falls are best reached from Upper Foyers. The gorge descending into the Foyers River is narrow, wooded and very attractive.

❶ Start at the car park next to the post office. Cross the road to the gate at the start of the walk.

❷ From the gate follow the signs 'Falls of Foyers', first to the Upper Viewpoint, then down to the Lower Viewpoint. From the Lower Viewpoint retrace your steps, passing the Upper Viewpoint, to a signposted junction.

❸ Take the path signposted 'To Path Network and Lower Foyers'. Keep to the main path, always going downhill. At a clump of rhododendrons there is another signpost.

❹ Take the 'Lower Foyers/Loch Ness' path (blue marker post). Stay on the main path; it eventually ends at a tarred road. If you go on to the lochside, return here. Retracing your steps you come to a wooden bridge over a pipeline.

❺ Cross the bridge and go left, up a few steps, to a junction. Turn left here for a few metres. Cross a wooden bridge and immediately turn right and retrace your steps to the car park.

further information

At Step 4, you can extend the walk by going on into Lower Foyers, on the lochside (this is one of the best areas for spotting the famous Loch Ness Monster!).

access information

Approach Foyers on the B852 from Inverness. Take the Upper Foyers road 1.5 km before Foyers. Park at the small car park next to the post office, on the main road. There is a limited bus service from Inverness to Foyers.

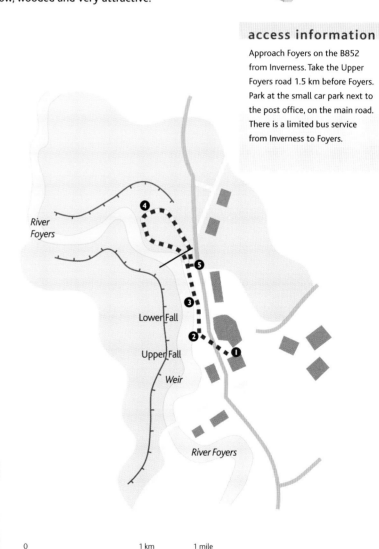

▲ Map: Explorer 416
▲ Distance: 5 km/3 miles
▲ Walk ID: 1437 D. B. Grant

Difficulty rating

Time

▲ Hills or Fells, Loch, Pub, Toilets, Play Area, Wildlife, Birds, Flowers, Great Views, Butterflies, Good for Kids, Tea Shop, Woodland

Loch Ness.

Aldourie from Dores

A short circular walk at the northern end of Loch Ness which goes partly along the loch shore and partly along a ridge. You can see Loch Ness from one end to the other.

❶ Cross the B862 at the Dores Inn and go through the gate. Beyond the green shed there is a narrow path leading to the children's playpark. Follow this lochside path, passing many viewpoints. Continue to reach the entry to a wood.

❷ From the wood go down to the beach, where there is a good path, and follow it for 400 m, passing Tor Point, to a turn off on your right. This path goes to a higher level and follows the loch for a while before joining the main forestry track.

❸ On the main track go left, to arrive at the pier and anchorage. At the pier take the path leading off right. Follow this path uphill to a T-junction.

❹ Turn right and continue to a fork. At the fork go left. The track follows a fence for a while, to a viewpoint. Continue, to a grassy fork.

❺ Take the left fork here, downhill. Here you will find a good view to Dores.

❻ After about 200 m there is a mini-crossroads. Go left, downhill, and head back to the car park at Dores.

access information

Dores lies 13 km south-west of Inverness, on the junction of the B862 and the B852. Park opposite the Dores Inn. If you wish to use public transport, there is a bus service from Inverness.

Aldourie Castle

Pier

Strath Dore

Strath Dore

An Torr

Tor Point

Loch Ness

Dores

B862

0   1 km   1 mile

▲ Map: Explorer 433

▲ Distance: 6 km/3¾ miles

▲ Walk ID: 827 D. B. Grant

Difficulty rating

Time

▲ Hills or Fells, River, Sea, Pub, Stately Home, Wildlife, Birds, Flowers, Great Views, Butterflies, Food Shop, Good for Kids, Moor, Waterfall

Flowerdale Falls from Gairloch

This pleasant family walk goes from sea level at Gairloch to 150 m at the falls. The walk can be made shorter by returning the same way, but the alternative return route offers splendid views of hills and sea.

❶ From the car park take the gravel path leading upstream. It soon joins a road to Flowerdale House. After passing the house there is a T-junction.

❷ At the T-junction turn right. Go straight on to reach Flowerdale Mains (trekking centre). Here go through the gate and continue on this path to a three-way junction. Keep straight on, following the red posts, to reach the falls. At the falls cross the bridge and take the narrow path up the side of the falls. At the top go on for 200 m to another wooden bridge.

❸ Cross the bridge and follow the path downhill to a junction. If you want to go back to the car park quickly go right, and return by the outward route; to continue on this walk turn left, uphill, for a kilometre to a wooden bridge.

❹ Cross the bridge and follow the narrow but delightful path for a short way, well marked with blue posts. When you reach the lowest point on the path, cross the little burn at the blue post and go left for 20 m.

❺ Here you will see two blue markers on your right, marking a faint track going uphill to a viewpoint. You may either go up to the viewpoint or carry on along the lower path; the two paths soon meet again. Continue on this path to a T-junction with a main path.

❻ At the junction turn right and go through the double wooden gates. Shortly, you arrive at a DIY store. Pass it and immediately go right. You should now be at the Old Inn, by the car park.

Gairloch is one of the most glorious and unspoilt wilderness regions in the whole of Britain.

access information

Charlestown (Gairloch) is on the A832. The car park is opposite the pier at the mouth of the river, conveniently by The Old Inn.

Gairloch

A832

Kinloc

Flowerdale is a glen sheltered from most winds. It has a microclimate of its own, supporting plants such as bog orchids, bog asphodels, butterwort and sundew. Animals and birds such as voles, pine martens, stoats, weasels and buzzards can also be seen.

This bridge above Flowerdale Falls is as far as you go as you follow the footpath upstream.

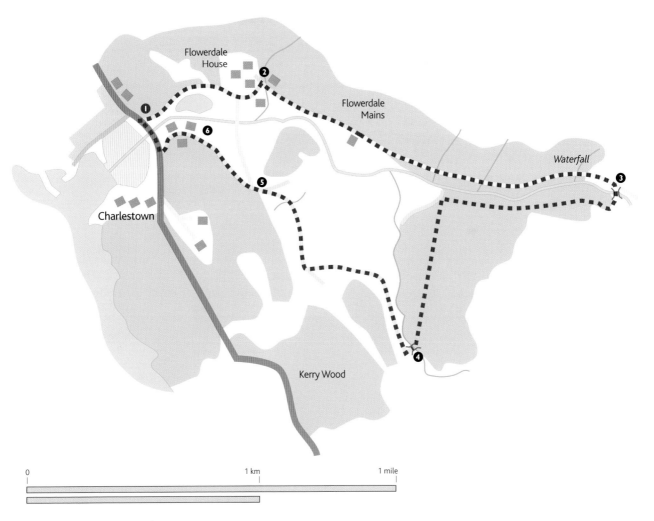

Flowerdale House

Flowerdale Mains

Waterfall

Charlestown

Kerry Wood

0　　　　　　　　　1 km　　　　　　　1 mile

Woodland & Hillside

Scotland's woodland and hillside footpaths reveal soaring highlands, sweeping glens and forests, and ancient monuments. Highlights include Arthur's Seat, Edin's Hall Broch and Abernethy Forest.

▲ Map: Explorer 350
▲ Distance: 6 km/3¾ miles
▲ Walk ID: 110 Oliver O'Brien

Difficulty rating

🐾🐾🐾

Time

⬤⬤

▲ Hills or Fells, Lake/Loch, Toilets, Church, Stately Home, Great Views

Arthur's Seat in Holyrood Park

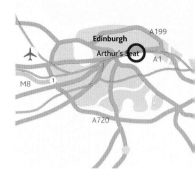

A tour of the small but picturesque royal estate of Holyrood Park, in the heart of Edinburgh, climbing one of the city's Seven Hills – Arthur's Seat.

1 From the west (city centre) end of the car park, cross the road and climb a small flight of stairs. Turn right, and climb steeply on a good path with the crags (Salisbury Crags) on your left and dramatic views quickly opening up on your right. Follow the path to the end of the crags.

2 Before you get to the road, turn left and follow a smaller path, rising up slightly and over a brow. Take any of several paths down the broad, flat valley, going to the left of the water/marsh at the centre. Turn left and pass to the right of some small crags, then climb steeply but briefly uphill on a small path, aiming just to the right of the chapel remains.

3 Walk left to visit the chapel. Then turn back and follow a good path first back the way you came, walking straight ahead. Continue along the path into a smaller valley, parallel to the previous one. Follow the path up the right-hand side. The summit of Arthur's Seat is straight ahead. Continue up the path, climbing more steeply. The path peters out as it joins the main 'tourist' route up to Arthur's Seat. Turn right and follow it up.

4 On a fine day the views from the summit are magnificent. Turn back and head back down the tourist route, on a stepped path. Carry on straight down the tourist route, which becomes wide and grassy. Head down to Dunsapie Loch. Turn left and walk alongside the loch or follow a path around the left-hand side of the small hill.

5 Meet the path beside the road. Carry on down beside the road, to the bottom.

6 Take a small path to the left just after the set of barrier gates on the road. Follow this path around the left-hand side of the loch. Come back onto the road and walk back to the start.

Arthur's Seat is an extinct volcano in the heart of Edinburgh from where you have superb views of the city.

access information

The start of the walk is opposite the west end of the Palace of Holyroodhouse visitor car park. It is also a 10-minute walk from Edinburgh's central Waverley Station. From here, head out of the north-east entrance and follow the road east to the Palace of Holyroodhouse, then south. By bus the start is a 10 to 15-minute walk from St Andrew's Square, Edinburgh's main bus station. Head south and climb to the High Street, then walk down the Royal Mile to the Palace of Holyroodhouse.

further information

Holyrood Park is a huge royal park open to the public. It is adjacent to the Palace of Holyroodhouse – Her Majesty the Queen's official residence in Scotland.

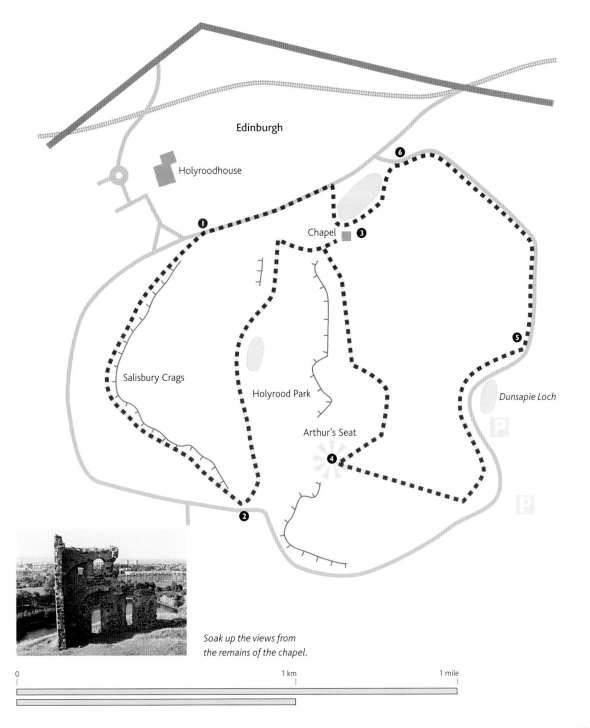

Edinburgh

Holyroodhouse

①

Chapel **③**

Salisbury Crags

Holyrood Park

Arthur's Seat

②

④

⑤

⑥

Dunsapie Loch

*Soak up the views from
the remains of the chapel.*

0   1 km   1 mile

▲ Map: Explorer 344

▲ Distance: 11 km/6¾ miles

▲ Walk ID: 10 John Stewart

Difficulty rating

Time

▲ Hills or Fells, Lake/Loch, Pub, Toilets, Great Views

The Pentland Hills

This walk lies in the heart of the peaceful Pentland Hills, just a few kilometres south of the hustle and bustle of Edinburgh.

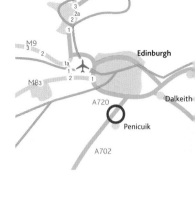

1 Take the path leading down the left-hand side of the Visitor Centre and follow it through the trees until it merges with the road.

2 Continue along the road, skirting the reservoir and stream on the left. After passing a house with an adjacent white-posted gate, a second reservoir can be seen. At the far end of the second reservoir, make for a white house and cross the stream by the wooden bridge. Turn right onto a path in front of the house, entering a small field beyond.

3 Walk towards the far left corner of the field and cross a stile adjacent to a wooden gate onto a well-defined track. Follow the steepish path upwards across several stiles, making for the saddle in the ridge just beyond. The path flattens out onto a broad ridge and soon crosses a well-defined ridgeway track.

4 Turn left onto this track towards higher ground. Follow the track, which is fairly steep in parts, until you reach a large stone cairn surrounded by a stonefield. This is the highest point of the walk.

5 Continue on the track running slowly downwards from the cairn until you reach a new ridgeway saddle. Cross the stile and continue on the path towards the top of the hill straight ahead, where there is a small stone cairn. From here, you can see most of the path leading all the way back down to the start of the walk.

6 Follow the path down from the cairn through grassy slopes. Carry on towards the start of the walk among the trees beyond. The track finally descends to the stream on the left. Cross the wooden bridge onto the road and turn right to reach the Visitor Centre and the car park.

On a clear day, you get marvellous views of the whole area from the top of the Pentland Hills – a chain of small, dome-shaped hills.

access information

The start of the walk is most easily reached by car. Take the main Edinburgh/Carlisle A702(T) road south out of the city to reach the Flotterstone Inn, which lies on the right side of the road about 5 km south of where the A702(T) crosses the Edinburgh by-pass (A720). Parking is available among the trees beyond the Inn and adjacent to the Visitor Centre.

Every August, Edinburgh Castle hosts a famous Military Tattoo within its walls.

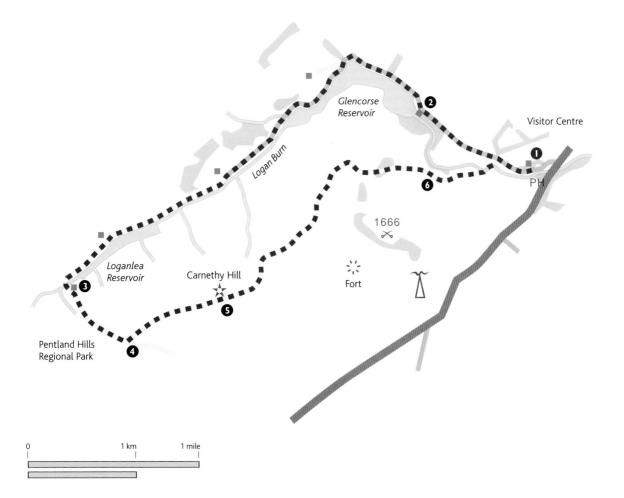

▲ Map: Explorer 346

▲ Distance: 10 km/6¼ miles

▲ Walk ID: 121 Oliver O'Brien

Difficulty rating

Time

▲ Hills or Fells, River, Toilets, Church, Stately Home, Wildlife, Flowers, Great Views

Edin's Hall Broch from Abbey St Bathans

This scenic circular walk starts and finishes at Abbey St Bathans, an historic estate village. Along the route there is a medieval broch, two suspension bridges, profuse oak woodlands, and a moorland, all in a 10 km walk!

You cross Whiteadder Water a couple of times on spectacular suspension bridges.

1 Follow the road south-east through the village. Continue, bearing right and climbing. Take the small path that starts here to the left of the road and runs for a short way through woodland, before rejoining the road.

2 The road turns sharp right. Take the path left dropping steeply to a stream. Cross the bridge and follow the path, gradually climbing. Turn left and go down beside a field. At the end of the field, turn right, and follow the path up, climbing steeply.

3 Pass Edin's Hall Broch (the well-preserved medieval fort) to its right, then bear left slightly to pick up a well-defined path going steeply down the hill, through a gate. After crossing a wall with stone steps turn sharp left. Turn right at the bottom of the field, staying on top of a ridge above the river's flat flood plain. Follow it round to the right. At a small junction bear left into a thicket.

4 Cross the gate and follow the path to the left passing some cottages on your right. Cross the suspension bridge above Whiteadder Water. Follow the track on the other side, through open land and then through a forest, passing two signposts. Turn left onto a very quiet country road, and follow it uphill.

5 At the junction turn left, cross over a stile and follow a track beside a field, crossing two gates and gradually dropping down into a valley. At a signpost join the Southern Upland Way. Turn left and follow the track. Cross the gate and continue on the track.

6 At Whiteadder Water turn sharp right (signposted) and follow a small path with the river on your left. Turn left off the path and cross a large and very long suspension bridge and back to the start.

access information

From the north take the A1 to Cockburnspath, then follow unclassified roads south and uphill, signposted to Abbey St Bathans. From the south take the A1 to Grantshouse, turn off left (S) on to the A6112 for 10 km to Reston, turn right (W) on to the B6355 for 4 km, then right (N) onto an unclassified road signposted to Abbey St Bathans. There is no regular public service to Abbey St Bathans – the nearest access by bus is at Grantshouse on the A1 – 6 km north of the halfway point of this walk. Start by the village church, opposite a red phone box.

further information

Much of the walk is signposted by small yellow arrows (for the first part) or Long Distance Path markers (for the last section).

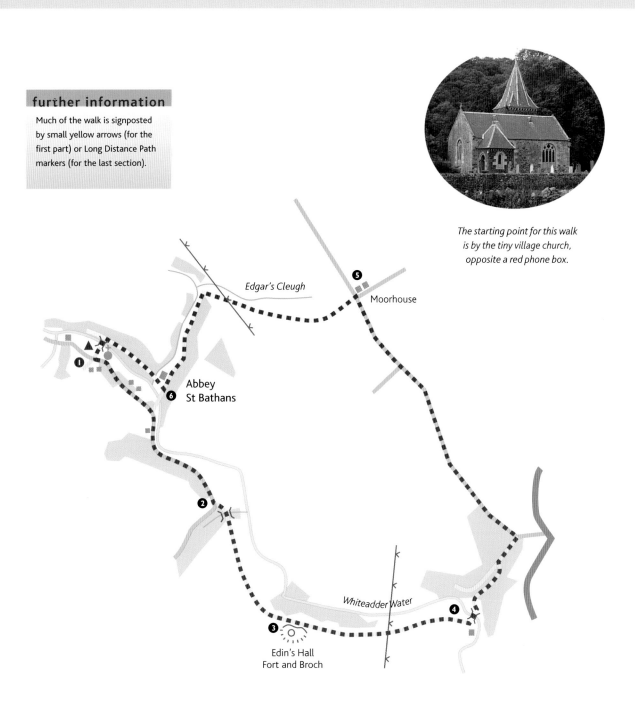

The starting point for this walk is by the tiny village church, opposite a red phone box.

Edgar's Cleugh

5 Moorhouse

1

▲

Abbey
St Bathans

6

2

Whiteadder Water

4

3
Edin's Hall
Fort and Broch

0   1 km   1 mile

▲ Map: Explorer 326

▲ Distance: 5 km/3 miles

▲ Walk ID: 1201 Jude Howat

Difficulty rating

Time

▲ River, Wildlife, Birds, Flowers, Great Views, Butterflies

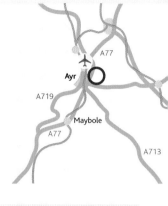

Wallace's Seat from Oswald's Bridge

The first part of this very pleasant walk follows the river through trees. At the turning point there is a seat by the river to enjoy the view (supposedly where William Wallace sat and contemplated his fight with the English).

1 Turn left to cross the bridge over the river. Turn immediately left at the post with the green robin sign and descend the stairs to the riverbank. The path is clear and takes you through some trees.

2 A steep climb leads to the top of Three Knights Field to a viewpoint. At this point admire the view – on a clear day you can see as far as the Isle of Arran. Continue to follow the green robin waymarks.

3 The green robin route crosses the stile here but this walk continues to the left, this time following red robin signposts which follow the path through Pheasant Nook Wood. Continue through Craighall Wood until high above the river where Wallace's Seat can be seen.

4 There are steps down to the seat to enjoy the view. When you leave the river, care should be taken to double back. The path continues along the river but as you walk away from the river you should see a narrow path which turns back in the direction you have come. Stay close to the fence until you meet the obvious cart track on the left.

5 Turn to the left out of the woods and walk along the broader cart track between fields and enjoy the pastoral views over Louden Law.

6 Climb over the stile, turn right and you are back to the start. If you wish you can enter Leglen Wood opposite and visit the monument to William Wallace.

River Ayr.

access information

Leave the A77 at the Heathfield roundabout, on the Ayr bypass, to take the B743 towards Auchencruive. After a kilometre take the minor road to the right labelled SAC Auchencruive, Leglen Wood. Just before Oswald's Bridge take the road to the left and park. If this car park is busy there is further parking closer to Oswald Hall.

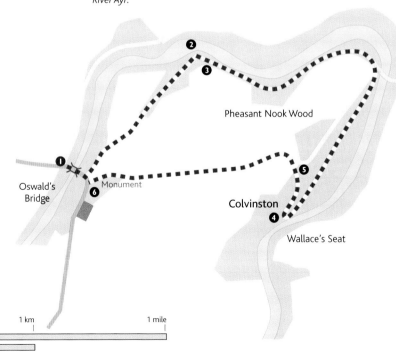

Pheasant Nook Wood

Oswald's Bridge

Monument

Colvinston

Wallace's Seat

0   1 km   1 mile

▲ Map: Explorer 326

▲ Distance: 4 km/2½ miles

▲ Walk ID: 902 J. & D. Howat

Difficulty rating

Time

▲ River, Pub, Toilets, Play Area, Church, Wildlife, Birds, Flowers, Great Views, Butterflies, Food Shop

Lambdoughty Glen from Straiton

This walk goes along a country road followed by a picturesque scramble up one side of a fast-flowing burn and back on the other side, with wonderful views of waterfalls, before returning to the picturesque village of Straiton.

❶ At the start of the walk follow the green arrows. Go straight on to the path at the end of the road and follow it until you reach the burn. Cross by the bridge. Turn to the left onto the road. The road goes uphill for about half a kilometre, passing Largs Farm.

❷ Turn to the left at the end of the trees to enter Lambdoughty Glen. A green arrow shows the way. The path to the left is easy to follow, with steps cut in the earth, held in place by boards, and a bridge to cross the burn.

❸ At the bridge you recross the burn and see the largest fall of all (known as the Rossetti Linn because the painter Dante Gabriel Rossetti was thought to have contemplated suicide here). Continue on the high path, now fairly level.

❹ Turn right onto the road again as you leave the wood and walk back as far as the wooden bridge, to Straiton. Turn right at the T-junction. Continue past the church and back to the car park or parking place.

access information

From the A77 south of Ayr take the B7045 to Kirkmichael and on to Straiton. Park on the right or in the car park.

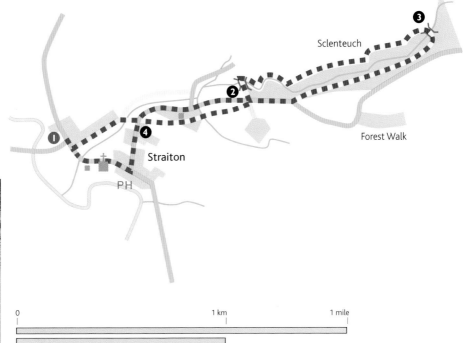

The grandest fall on your route is known as the Rossetti Linn, after the Pre-Raphaelite painter Dante Gabriel Rossetti, who is believed to have contemplated suicide at this point.

0   1 km   1 mile

▲ Map: Explorer 407
▲ Distance: 9 km/5½ miles
▲ Walk ID: 1067 C. & J. Simpson

Difficulty rating

Time

▲ Hills or Fells, Mountains, Sea, Great Views, Moor

Macleod's Tables from Osdale

This circular route is over the two hills, known as Macleod's Tables (North and South), that dominate the north west of Skye. The isolated location of the hills means they have excellent views to the Outer Hebrides.

1 From the B884 Dunvegan to Glendale road follow the track through the gate towards the ruin at Osdale.

2 Pass by the ruin and start to head uphill behind it. To pick up a path of sorts, head uphill to the corner of the fence on your left and cross a little stream just beyond it. Continue uphill to a gorge and follow its right-hand side until you can cross it. Head up through a hollow to the more open slopes to the top of the hill.

3 The summit of Healabhal Mhor (Macleod's Table North) is towards the far side of the flat summit plateau and is marked by a cairn.

4 To continue to the south table, walk south for about 200 m, after which there is a fairly abrupt drop towards a flattish col and the ridge leading to Healabhal Bheag (Macleod's Table South). The descent is easier than it looks. Beyond the col is a more obvious ridge over the small top and onwards to the climb up the south table.

5 The summit of Healabhal Bheag is marked by a trig point and a cairn. Continue north-east past the second cairn until you see a prominent ridge which is followed for a few hundred metres. This ends in a prominent steep nose so you should descend the easier slopes on your left as you continue to follow the line of the ridge.

6 After dropping off the side of the ridge you can pick your own line – heading for the Osdale River, which is followed downstream. The best return route is to keep fairly close to the river until it begins to meander quite widely and then take an obvious direct route back to the road.

Your reward for reaching the summit is the stunning view over Loch Dunvegan, but it is safer to be off the hills by sunset.

access information

The starting point is about 2 km along the B884 road from Dunvegan, just beyond the bridge over the Osdale River. There is plenty of parking, particularly near the bridge. Public transport is limited, although the walk could easily be done from Dunvegan without the need for a car.

further information

There is another cairn, where there are better views, about 100 m north-east of the summit of Healabhal Bheag.

B884

❶

Osdale

❷

❸

Healabhal Mhor
(Macleod's Table
North)

❹

Glen Osdale

Osdale River

This is the sort of rugged countryside you can expect to be covering on this hill walk.

Healabhal Bheag
(Macleod's Table South)

❺

❻

0   1 km   1 mile

North-east England

Coastal & Waterside

Waterside walks in North-east England unveil the coasts of Durham and Northumberland, and Yorkshire's scenic bays and reservoirs. Highlights include Beal Sands and Grassington.

▲ Map: Explorer 340

▲ Distance: 16 km/10 miles

▲ Walk ID: 507 H. Weightman

Difficulty rating

👣👣

Time

●●●●◖

▲ Pub, Church, Castle, Birds, Great Views

Holy Island from Beal Sands

This walk crosses the vast Goswick Sands to reach Holy Island by The Snook, then continues to the village and castle to return by the Pilgrim's Way. Before you start, be sure to note the information about tides and observe the warnings.

❶ From the parking area, follow the footpath, skirting Beal Point to enter the estuary. Cross the dyke, turn right and pass over the sluice-bridge, before continuing along a raised track towards the prominent tower by Beachcomber Farm. At the tower, turn right and head through the dunes to the beach. Walk for 600 m towards the shoreline.

❷ Turn diagonally right and cross the sands to Lindisfarne, heading towards a small tower (The Snook). After about 1 km wade across the watercourse, or follow the bank for 200 m for an easier crossing.

❸ At the Snook, check the time – it should have taken no more than 2 hours to reach this point. Pass to the left of the farm buildings and continue down the track to meet the causeway. Turn left to reach the village. Just past the sign to the Lindisfarne Hotel turn left and head towards the harbour.

❹ At the harbour, take in the fine views of the castle, the Farne Islands and Bamburgh. Follow the path to the castle. After visiting the castle, return to the shore. Climb by the path to the left and follow it left around a field border.

❺ Turn left at the signpost, following the path back to the village. Retrace your steps to reach the causeway.

❻ This is the start of the Pilgrim's Way. Do not attempt this crossing less than

3 hours before the end of safe crossing time posted on the tide tables. Follow the line of the poles if conditions are right, or follow the causeway, remembering that this, too, will be impassable after the safe crossing time. Both routes end at the start point of this walk.

access information

Road access is signed from the A1 south of Berwick-upon-Tweed. There is no public transport to the island.

further information

IMPORTANT: This walk involves two crossings of tidal areas that are submerged to a depth of 2 m at high tide. The most comprehensive tide information is available from www.northumberland.gov.uk/vg/tidetabl.html.

Along the coast from Holy Island, Bamburgh Castle stands on an ancient rocky outcrop overlooking kilometres of beautiful sandy beach.

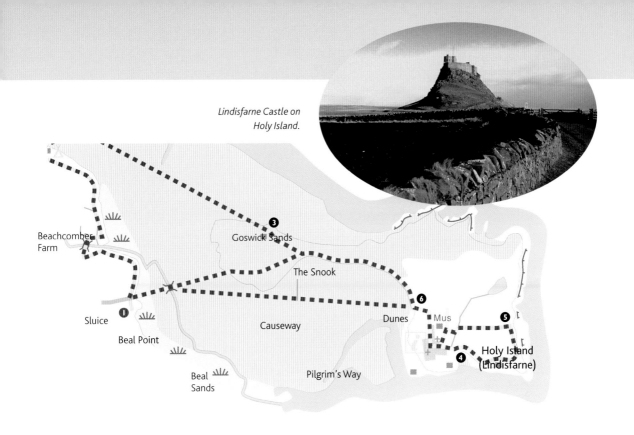

Lindisfarne Castle on
Holy Island.

Beachcomber
Farm

Goswick Sands ❸

The Snook

Sluice ❶

Dunes ❻

Mus

❺

Beal Point

Causeway

Pilgrim's Way

❹

Holy Island
(Lindisfarne)

Beal
Sands

0   1 km   1 mile

▲ Map: Explorer 316
▲ Distance: 10.6 km/6½ miles
▲ Walk ID: 724 Jude Howat

Difficulty rating

Time

▲ Sea, Pub, Toilets, Museum, Birds, Great Views

St Mary's Island from Tynemouth

This coastal walk begins at Tynemouth and heads through the popular resort of Whitley Bay to reach St Mary's Island where, tides permitting, you can visit the lighthouse via a causeway. The walk returns along the headland.

① From the car park, cross the road and head north along the promenade, past Cullercoats Bay. Keep to the pavement until you reach the clock.

② Take the steps to the lower level and head for the slipway down to the beach. Walk along the beach towards the lighthouse (St Mary's Island). At the far end of the bay, take the steps and then the path. Tides permitting, cross the causeway to visit the lighthouse. Return via the causeway.

③ After crossing the causeway, continue straight ahead and follow the road for a short distance. There is a nature reserve to the right, just beyond the car park. As the road bends sharply to the right, leave it and take the path to the left. This path is not shown as a public footpath on the map but is well used.

④ There are many paths coming in from the right along the coast – ignore all of these and continue straight ahead. When you reach the hump-backed bridge, cross over to continue for a short distance along the coastal footpath.

⑤ Take the left-hand path, towards the sea again. This takes you down to the lower level of the promenade. After a short distance you will see a path heading back up the dunes. Take this path to continue past a small outdoor auditorium. Take the left-hand fork along the coast.

⑥ Towards the end of the bay, the promenade paths come to an end. Rejoin the promenade alongside the road. Retrace your steps along the coast and back towards the start point.

further information

St Mary's Island has a lighthouse, which was built in 1898 and remained operational until 1984. The island is now run as a visitor centre, with the surrounding area maintained as a nature reserve. It is advisable to check the tide table for the area before commencing this walk.

Tel: 0191 200 8650

Ideally, this walk should be done at low tide so that you can cross the causeway to visit the lighthouse on St Mary's Island.

St Mary's Island

PC

access information

Parking is available along the shore at Tynemouth, close to the church. From Newcastle follow the A1058 to Tynemouth/Cullercoats. At the coastal roundabout turn left and the parking is about 200 m on the left. Alternatively, take the metro to Cullercoats station, and walk the short distance to the coast.

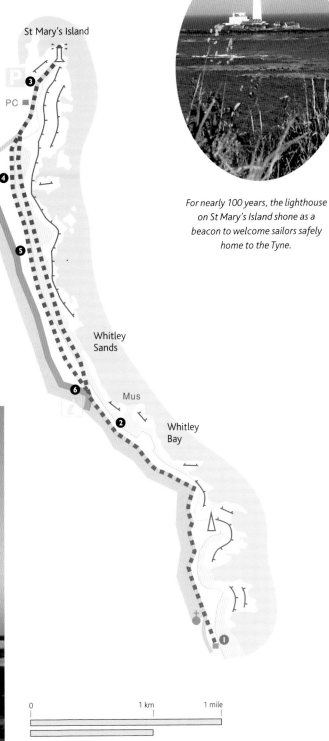

For nearly 100 years, the lighthouse on St Mary's Island shone as a beacon to welcome sailors safely home to the Tyne.

Whitley Sands

Mus

Whitley Bay

0   1 km   1 mile

▲ Map: Explorer OL 31
▲ Distance: 6 km/3¾ miles
▲ Walk ID: 320 Jude Howat

Difficulty rating

Time

▲ Hills, Wildlife, Lake, Waterfall,
Nature Trail

Cauldron Snout from Cow Green Reservoir

This is the easy way to see the beautiful Cauldron Snout waterfalls. The walk follows the Teesdale National Nature Reserve nature trail, which is on a tarmac path along the side of the reservoir.

1 Leave the car park and walk 300 m back along the road. At the marker turn right and follow the beginning of the nature trail. If you have a wheelchair with you, continue on the road for a further 400 m, then turn right. These routes will rejoin each other.

2 When the narrow path reaches a T-junction with a wider path, turn left. Continue on this path, then take the tarmac path and go straight on. Pass through the stile, which is wide enough for a wheelchair. Follow the track along the side of the reservoir.

3 Continue straight ahead, ignoring the junction to the right. Just before a small bridge over the river you will see a path off to the left. The path is a bit of a scramble and the rocks can be very slippery – this is the only part of the walk that is not suitable for wheelchairs. The path leads you to the waterfalls.

4 After enjoying views of Cauldron Snout, return by the same route to the car park.

further information

Come prepared for chilly, wet, windy weather as the hills are very exposed and even in summer it can be very cold. The route is good for wheelchairs, but the path to the waterfalls is not accessible.

access information

Follow the B6282 from Middleton-in-Teesdale past High Force. Turn left at Langdon Beck. Follow signs to Cow Green Reservoir.

Teesdale offers some of the most beautiful rolling countryside in England.

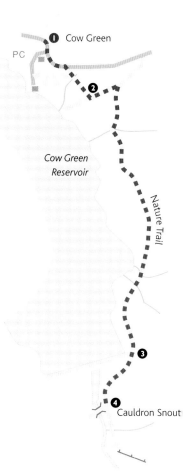

▲ Map: Explorer OL 43
▲ Distance: 2.5 km/1½ miles
▲ Walk ID: 592 Jude Howat

Difficulty rating

Time

▲ River, Pub, Great Views

Blanchland Circular Walk

From the picturesque village of Blanchland this walk takes you through the village square to reach the River Derwent. The narrow path then picks its way along the river to return to the village via a short section of road.

❶ Leaving the car park, turn right and walk into the square in the centre of the village. Pass under a stone arch and continue through the square to reach the bridge over the River Derwent. Do not cross the bridge.

❷ Just before the bridge, take the public footpath, then join the riverside path. Turn left at the river bank and follow the path along the river.

❸ Cross the double stile and continue along the river bank, passing an old barn in the fields to the left. Just after the barn, fork left to join a farm track. Follow the track, first up the hill and then left, along the hillside.

❹ On reaching the road, keep straight ahead and continue along the hillside and down into the village again. At the old village church, turn right to return to the car park.

Even the bubbly young River Derwent at Blanchland runs out of gurgle during a dry spell.

access information

Blanchland is off the A68, on the B6278 to Blanchland and Edmundbyers.

Blanchland

Abbey

River Derwent

0   1 km   1 mile

▲ Map: Explorer OL 21
▲ Distance: 5 km/3 miles
▲ Walk ID: 1104 Barry Smith

Difficulty rating

Time

▲ Lake, Wildlife, Great Views,
Ancient Monument, Good for Kids

Oxygrains from Ripponden

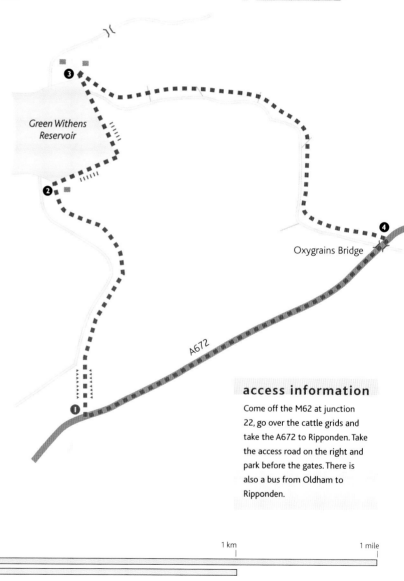

Green Withens Reservoir.

This short walk takes in Green Withens Clough and Oxygrains, with two bridges at the far end on the A672. A gentle climb back up the road takes you back to your car.

❶ Cross the road to the gates with the sign for Green Withens Reservoir. Go through a stone stile with a signpost, leading to the top of the hill. Where the tarmac road turns into a gravel track, bear right. Continue to Green Withens Reservoir Sailing Club.

❷ At the sailing club car park, go right through a large gate and continue on the reservoir embankment. Bear left at the corner, passing Green Withens Clough.

❸ Just after passing a solar panel there is a signposted path to the right, directing the walk to Oxygrains Bridge. Take the path next to the run-off channel, not the one that the sheep are on. Descend on the path and down some steps.

❹ After dropping down the valley, through Green Withens Clough and Oxygrains, you will emerge at the exit onto the A672. Turn right and follow the road back to the car.

further information

Oxygrains Bridge crosses a tributary stream to the River Ryburn at Rishworth. The stream flows down to Booth Wood Reservoir via the much smaller Spa Clough and Booth Dean reservoirs. The name Oxygrains comes from 'Osc', which is an old word for water, and 'grains', referring to the joining of two streams.

Green Withens Reservoir

Oxygrains Bridge

A672

access information

Come off the M62 at junction 22, go over the cattle grids and take the A672 to Ripponden. Take the access road on the right and park before the gates. There is also a bus from Oldham to Ripponden.

0   1 km   1 mile

▲ Map: Explorer OL 31
▲ Distance: 9.5 km/6 miles
▲ Walk ID: 33 Maggie Davey

Difficulty rating

Time

▲ River, Wildlife, Castle, Pub

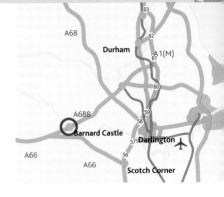

Lartington Hall from Barnard Castle

This delightful walk follows the River Tees, a section of disused railway and some woodland to reach Lartington Hall. The Hall has fascinating medieval field systems, protected under the Countryside Stewardship Scheme.

❶ From Barnard Castle cross the bridge over the Tees and then take the B6277 towards Lartington. Just after the bridge, turn left onto the track alongside the stream. Cross the bridge over a small stream and bear left, back towards the river. Then take the path on the right.

❷ Follow the path up the hill. Join a track, which leads to the Deepdale Viaduct. Just beyond the viaduct, turn right onto the path. Follow the disused railway line, passing the old signal box. Turn right onto the road and walk down through Lartington village.

❸ Take the left fork and continue to Lartington Hall. Walk down the drive, which leads to the back of the Hall. Keep on the road as it goes past a small outbuilding, and follow the sign to Barnard Castle. Go through the gate and follow the path along the stream. Turn left, cross the bridge and continue up the road.

❹ Just above the caravan site, turn right over the stile. Follow the path into the woods. The path emerges next to a cottage. Turn right onto the track, back towards Barnard Castle.

further information

Deepdale Viaduct was a magnificent steel structure which spanned the valley – it was taken down following the Beeching Report in 1963.

access information

Barnard Castle is a short distance along the A66 from Scotch Corner.

While in the area, take time to explore the ruins of Barnard Castle.

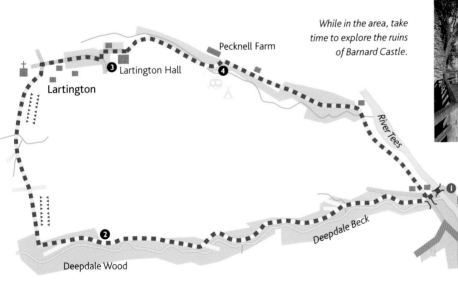

0   1 km   1 mile

▲ Map: Explorer OL 2

▲ Distance: 11 km/7 miles

▲ Walk ID: 113 L. and D. Fishlock

Difficulty rating

Time

▲ Hills or Fells, River, Pub, Toilets, Wildlife, Birds, Flowers, Great Views

Linton and Burnsall from Grassington

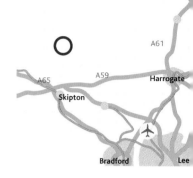

This undemanding walk takes you through the delightful little villages of Burnsall and Linton, ending with a visit to the beautiful Linton waterfall to complete a truly enjoyable family day out.

❶ Go through the gate at the back of the car park. Turn right, following the sign to Linton Falls. At the junction before Linton Falls, turn left onto the riverside path. Follow the footpath sign away from the river to a stile onto the lane. Turn right.

❷ At the junction, follow the signed footpath to Burnsall. Cross a field, a footbridge and a kissing gate, to follow the river again. Turn right to cross the Hebden suspension bridge and then left towards Burnsall. Cross a stone stile to continue along the riverbank.

❸ Turn right before Burnsall Bridge. When the road turns right, take the left path, crossing a number of fields, lanes and stiles. Continue in the same direction, following the footpath signs and crossing Startan Beck. Go through the stile and straight on. Pass through a gate and exit the field through a stile in the corner. Turn left along the lane through Thorpe.

❹ Take the left fork. Continue along the lane, then cross a gated stile on your right. Follow the path through the field. Just after the footpath sign, continue ahead and cross the next stile and field. Go through the farmyard, then turn right along the road to enter Linton.

❺ At the T-Junction, turn left across the bridge and take the footpath on the right, along Linton Beck (signpost to

Threshfield). Follow the path to the right, in front of Linton Country Crafts and then between dry-stone walls. Take the right fork, continuing under the old railway bridge. Cross the field, over a small stream towards a small strip of woodland. Cross the main road. Take the path on your left to Threshfield School and turn right.

❻ Turn left along Church Road. Take the path on the left to Linton Falls. Turn right just before a small bridge and cross Linton Falls Bridge. Retrace the route to the car park.

access information

The walk starts from the National Park Information Centre just off the B6265 Grassington-Hebden road (fee payable). Bus services to the park operate from Leeds, Bradford and York.

Grassington is a charming village of traditional stone cottages and cobbled streets in Upper Wharfedale at the heart of the Yorkshire Dales National Park.

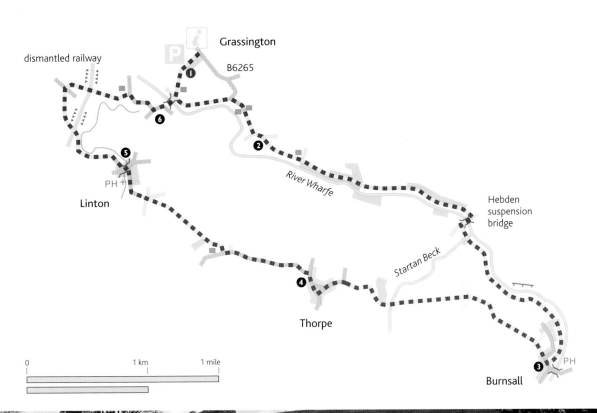

dismantled railway

Grassington

B6265

❶

❻

❷

River Wharfe

❺

PH

Linton

Hebden
suspension
bridge

Startan Beck

❹

Thorpe

❸

PH

Burnsall

0   1 km   1 mile

The woodland and hillside walks of North-east England reveal such wonders as Hadrian's Wall and the Yorkshire Dales. Highlights include Ilkley Moor, Simonside Crags and Hamsterley Forest.

▲ Map: Explorer OL 42

▲ Distance: 9.6 km/6 miles

▲ Walk ID: 427 Jude Howat

Difficulty rating

Time

●●●◖

▲ Hills or Fells, Great Views

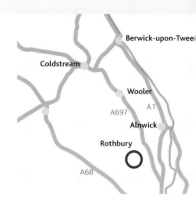

Simonside Crags from Lordenshaws

This is a wonderfully bracing ridge walk, which takes in the four peaks of The Beacon Cairn, Dove Crag, Simonside Crags and Lordenshaws Fort, with breathtaking views along the way.

❶ Follow the rocky footpath up the hill, and take the first right fork to continue towards The Beacon Cairn. The path follows a high-level ridge and offers superb views. Cross over the stile and continue uphill towards the summit of Dove Crag.

❷ Just before you reach the summit, take the left fork and follow the broad track which leads to a cairn. Continue along the ridge-top path. The path passes to the right of Old Stell Crag, leading to the summit directly above Simonside Crags. At the summit, descend via a steep path down the face of the crag to join a forest track.

❸ Turn right onto the track. It bends left sharply, then descends into the forest. At the marker, turn right. Pass by a bridge on the right and continue down the hill to reach a grassy picnic area.

❹ Aim diagonally right across the grass to join a short path, which leads to the road. Turn left onto the bridleway, just beyond the cattle grid, and head up a small hill. Past the quarry the path turns to the right, through a gate. Continue along the path, and through a further two gates, to reach Whitton Hillhead Farm. At the farm, turn right onto the farm track.

❺ At the next junction turn right. Follow the track up the hill to Whittondean and Lordenshaws Fort.

❻ Near the top of the hill, take the left path to go up to the fort (then retrace your steps to this point). Continue straight ahead to reach the car park.

The views around Rothbury include stunning panoramas of peaks, crags and rolling countryside.

access information

From Alnwick, follow the B6341 to Rothbury. In Rothbury take the left turn (just after the first village shop) to cross the river. Follow the road to the left and up over the moor. Take the signposted road to Lordenshaws car park.

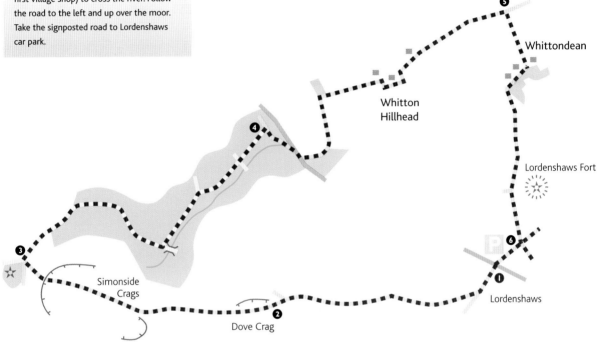

Whittondean

Whitton
Hillhead

Lordenshaws Fort

Simonside
Crags

Dove Crag

Lordenshaws

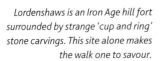

0   1 km   1 mile

Lordenshaws is an Iron Age hill fort surrounded by strange 'cup and ring' stone carvings. This site alone makes the walk one to savour.

▲ Map: Explorer 305
▲ Distance: 13 km/8 miles
▲ Walk ID: 498 Karen Land

Difficulty rating

Time

▲ River, Great Views

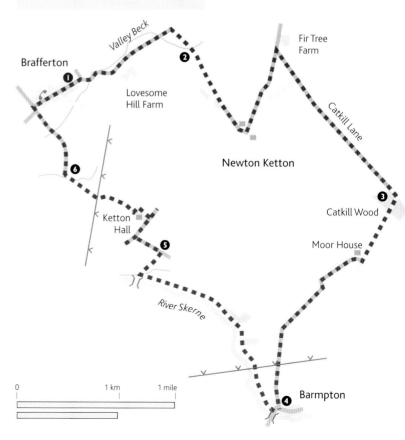

The kissing gate in front of Barmpton Hall.

Brafferton to Ketton Country

The village of Brafferton lies in a small area of rolling countryside steeped in history, known locally as 'Ketton Country'. The walk is an easy ramble along old tracks, green lanes and ancient highways of outstanding beauty.

❶ Walk up the main street. At the end, follow High House Lane across Valley Beck. Just before it bends left towards High House Farm, go through a field gate on the right. Walk ahead through the field along a tall hedge. Continue on to reach a signed farm gate and stile.

❷ Climb gently between the hedges. The lane descends through several gates to arrive at Newton Ketton. Turn left at the junction. Just before reaching Fir Tree Farm, turn right into the ancient Catkill Lane and continue for 2 km.

❸ Soon after the entrance into Catkill Wood, take the footpath on the right, to cut through dense scrub. Proceed straight on, through the fields. At Moor House, head to the left of the buildings and follow the farm track to Barmpton.

❹ Pass through a kissing gate in front of Barmpton Hall. Walk along the River Skerne until you reach the farm bridge, then bear right to reach the old Ketton packhorse bridge. Behind the bridge take the right fork.

❺ Turn left at the access road. At the top of the hill, turn right to pass Ketton Hall. Just beyond a small wood, locate a green farm gate on the left. Follow the wood away. When it ends, continue straight on and through the bridle gate. Follow the left boundary fence to go through another gate. Veer right and stay near the hedge over the next two fields.

❻ At the far corner of the last field a pair of gates leads onto a quiet green lane that heads back to Brafferton.

access information

Brafferton is on an unclassified road off the A167 north of Darlington. Roadside parking is available in the village. There is also a regular bus service.

▲ Map: Explorer OL 43
▲ Distance: 4.8 km/3 miles
▲ Walk ID: 686 Jude Howat

Difficulty rating

Time

▲ Hills or Fells, Pub, Toilets, Castle, Great Views

Thirlwall Castle from Walltown

This short circular walk takes in part of Hadrian's Wall (between Walltown Quarry and Thirlwall Castle) and part of the Pennine Way. The walk provides lovely views, with relatively little effort!

1 Leave the car park and walk along the road to the T-junction. Turn right and continue for about 200 m, looking for a stile on the left.

2 Cross the stile and follow the wall along the hillside to join a farm track, heading steeply down the hill to the Tipalt Burn.

3 Cross the burn via the footbridge and follow the track up the hill on the far side, passing Thirlwall Castle on the way. Continue through the farmyard. Shortly after the farmyard, take the right fork and follow the path to Wood House.

4 At the junction, branch to the right and follow the road downhill towards the burn again. Cross the burn via the stepping stones, then follow the sunken track to the left and uphill.

5 Turn right at the marker and head through the field towards the Low Old Shields farmhouse. Exit the field in its far left-hand corner, then pass between the

shed and main farm building. Continue through the farmyard to join the farm track at the front of the farmhouse. Follow the track uphill as it joins a rough road. Turn right as it becomes a proper road again, and follow the route back down towards waymark 2.

6 This time, turn left onto the path at the end of the quarry picnic site. Follow the path, which runs parallel to the road taken at the beginning of the walk. The path leads back towards the car park.

This gentle walk takes in sights ranging from Hadrian's Wall to Tipalt Burn.

access information

From the A69 Haltwhistle to Brampton road, take the B6318 to Greenhead. In Greenhead, turn right up a steep hill for a short distance, then take the first road on the left (signposted to Walltown Quarry). Follow the quarry signs (turning right after a short distance) to the car park.

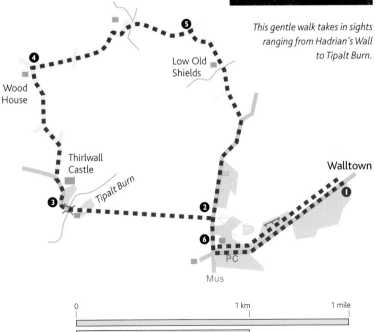

▲ Map: Explorer 304
▲ Distance: 9.5 km/6 miles
▲ Walk ID: 1034 M. Parkin

Difficulty rating

Time

▲ Wildlife, Birds, Great Views, Woodland

Whitcliffe Scar from Richmond

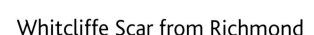

This tranquil walk passes through woods and fields above the River Swale, before returning along the heights of Whitcliffe Scar with enchanting views over Applegarth, Swaledale and Richmond.

1 Follow the track to High Leases and through Whitcliffe Wood. Stay on the track as it passes below Whitcliffe Scar, heading towards East Applegarth Farm. Continue straight ahead on a green track, passing through a gateway and a field. Cross the road and follow the path on the left. Cross the next road and the stile ahead. Cross another two fields and a small stream.

2 Head left to pass West Applegarth Farm. Follow the farm road, until it reaches the old Richmond to Reeth road. Turn right on Clapgate Bank and pass a junction for Whashton and Ravensworth. Cross the cattle grid on the right.

3 Almost immediately, leave the farm road, taking the green path to the left towards the top of Whitcliffe Scar. You will pass two monuments on the way. Carry on along the top of the scar. Keep to the breast of the hill for marvellous views of the Hambleton and Cleveland Hills and Richmond Castle.

4 Go down the hill to reach High Leases. Turn left along the track, back to the start of the walk.

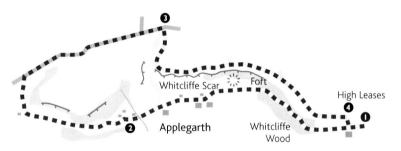

As you travel along Whitcliffe Scar, an enchanting view opens out before you.

access information

Heading out of Richmond on the main A6108 Reeth road, but before leaving the town at a sharp left, leave the main road and go up the avenue of West Fields. Follow the lane for just over a mile until the tarmac ends and park at the roadside between Whitcliffe and High Leases farms.

▲ Map: Explorer OL 31
▲ Distance: 3 km/2 miles
▲ Walk ID: 808 Jude Howat

Difficulty rating

Time

▲ River, Toilets, Play Area, Wildlife, Birds, Flowers, Great Views, Food Shop, Good for Kids, Tea Shop, Woodland

Hamsterley Forest from Bedburn

This short but enjoyable walk in Hamsterley Forest is ideal for when you need a breath of fresh air but time is limited. It takes you along both sides of the Bedburn Valley, through the forest, to return via the river.

1 Exit the car park via the small path leading into the forest. At the immediate T-junction turn right towards the children's play area, following the yellow markers. Turn left at the next T-junction to join the larger track. Cross over the burn (via a bridge) and follow the track uphill, into the forest. At the T-junction, turn right to follow the track along the hillside, until you reach a forest road.

2 Turn right, and descend for a short distance. Leave the road for the small path into the woods (signposted with a yellow marker). The path now begins to descend towards the river.

3 Do not cross the first bridge over the river. Instead, keep to the right and follow the path along the riverbank. The path does not follow the river, but meanders close by. Cross at the next bridge and turn right to follow the riverside path.

4 The adventure play area marks the end of the walk (the car park is just on its far side).

Both wild and arranged flowers add colour to the route as it heads off from Bedburn.

access information

Hamsterley Forest is close to the A68 near Bishop Auckland/Crook. There are brown tourist information signs from the junction close to Witton-le-Wear. Follow the signs, which lead into Hamsterley village. Keep following the signs through the village then out towards Bedburn. Park in the second car park.

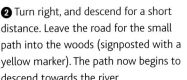

0   1 km   1 mile

▲ Map: Explorer 27
▲ Distance: 9 km/5½ miles
▲ Walk ID: 1019 Jean Hardman

Difficulty rating

!!!

Time

●●●◖

▲ Toilets, Birds, Great
Views, Moor, Ancient Monument

The Swastika Stone from Ilkley Town

Ilkley Moor is part of a large area of moorland, known collectively as Rombolds Moor. This walk explores the area around the Swastika Stone, mostly on good tracks and paths.

❶ Cross the road and walk up the steps to the paddling pool. Turn left along the path round the pool, then up the steps. Follow the tarmac path to the right of the shelter, then ahead up more steps and along a deeply rutted path towards the house. Take the steps down to the track, which heads downhill. Walk over the bridge and take the path to the left.

❷ Follow the path until it comes out onto the road. Turn left up the road for a short distance. At the signpost, turn right and cross over the footbridge. Follow the track along the moorside.

❸ Cross the bridge over Black Beck and continue ahead on the path alongside the wall. At the junction bear left away from the wall. Continue on the main path, crossing a series of three stone stiles and one wooden stile, taking in the extensive views across to Wharfedale. Just before the next wooden stile, take the narrow path on the left through the bracken to a stone stile. Go through the stile onto a path over the hill.

❹ At the wood, turn left and follow the path, keeping the wood on the right. When you reach the end of the wood, continue up past East Buck Stones, then on to Whetstone Gate.

❺ At Whetstone Gate, turn left and follow the wide stony track, passing Cowpers Cross on the left. Continue downhill for about 2 km until the track meets the road.

❻ Continue down the road, turn right at the junction and walk back to the car park.

further information

White Wells is a restored 18th-century bathhouse. It is open to visitors most weekends.

access information

There are regular bus and train services from Leeds to Ilkley. If using this form of transport you will need to add an extra 1.5 km to the distance for the walk up Wells Road and back down at the end of the walk.

By car take the A65 to Ilkley. At the traffic lights turn towards the B6382, turn left at the roundabout then first right up Wells Road, over the cattle grid at the top and immediately right into the large car park.

At Ilkley you will see not only the famous moor, but also these magnificent rock formations, the Cow and Calf Rocks.

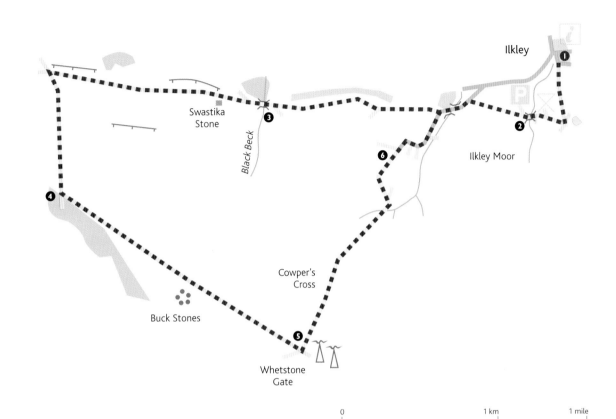

Ilkley

❶

❷

Swastika
Stone

❸

Black Beck

❻

Ilkley Moor

❹

Cowper's
Cross

Buck Stones

❺

Whetstone
Gate

0   1 km   1 mile

*The Swastika Stone is a magnificent
example of a Bronze Age swastika, or
follyfoot. The original is on the large
boulder, with a replica nearer the fence.
It is a version of the symbol of eternal life,
and dates from around 1800 BC.*

▲ Map: Explorer 27
▲ Distance: 8.5 km/5¼ miles
▲ Walk ID: 768 Jean Hardman

Difficulty rating

Time

▲ Great Views

Around Chevin Park

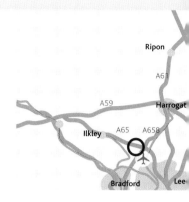

This is a favourite walk for weekend afternoons, with good tracks and superb views to Otley and Wharfedale. If you are lucky, you may spot some of the roe deer that live in Chevin Park – remember to keep dogs under control.

1 At the car park, go through the gap in the fence. Follow the path, bearing left to reach the main track. Turn right, then take the right fork along the broad track. Cross the stream, and take the right-hand track to the crest of the hill. Continue straight across the junction on a broad, sandy track. At the T-junction turn left, and head downhill. Bear left and go through the kissing gate. At the diverging paths keep straight ahead.

2 Turn left onto the main track and go through the gate. Follow the broad track to the top of Caley Crags. Continue straight ahead, then cross the bridge. Bear left over the walkway and follow the path on the right.

3 Take a small path to the right just before the car park, passing through a wooded area, running parallel with the road until you cross a stile. Turn right down the road, keeping to the verge, which becomes a footpath.

4 Cross the road and enter the East Chevin Quarry car park. At the far end, cross the stile and climb the broad track, which passes through the scrubland and then enters woodland. At the junction turn left. At the top turn right, keeping the woods on the right. Go straight ahead, passing the steps. Pass through a broken wall into a small wooded area. Follow the main path right and go through another broken wall.

5 Turn left at the junction, following the track uphill. At the top, turn left to reach the main path, and continue straight ahead. Take the next right-hand track, which goes above The Chevin with spectacular views. Continue past a car park.

6 Turn left at the gate and down the stony track to emerge on East Chevin Road. Cross the road and turn right to reach the car park.

A breathtaking view of Wharfedale on a glorious sunny day.

access information

Chevin Forest Park is south of the A660
Leeds to Otley road. If approaching from
Leeds, when you reach the junction with the
A658 (traffic lights at Dynley Arms), turn left
up the A658 and at the third right-hand
junction turn right onto East Chevin Road.
The car park is on the right.

*Beyond Caley Crags, the path
meanders over bridges and through
fields and forest.*

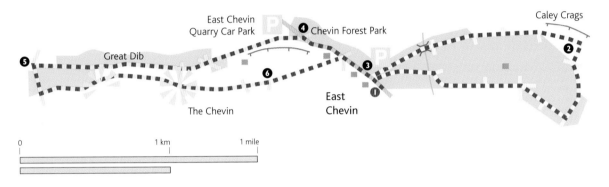

North-west England

Coastal & Waterside

The waterside walks of North-west England take in sea views and the inspirational calm of the Lake District. Highlights include Morecambe Bay, Elterwater and Buttermere.

▲ Map: Explorer 275
▲ Distance: 8 km/5 miles
▲ Walk ID: 256 Ian Darbyshire

Difficulty rating

Time

▲ River, Lake/Loch, Sea, Pub, Toilets, National Trust/NTS, Wildlife, Birds, Flowers, Great Views, Good for Wheelchairs

Hightown from Waterloo

This linear walk explores the seashore and sandhills that stretch between Waterloo Station, in the northern suburbs of Liverpool, and the Alt Estuary near Hightown. It is a rewarding route for bird-watching enthusiasts.

❶ Turn left from Waterloo Station and walk down South Road to the distant promenade, past the Marine Gardens. Follow the path to the right of Sefton Coastal Park. Go between the two lakes to reach the beach side of the promenade. Carry on up the path towards the promenade. Turn right and follow the promenade, either along the path or along the beach.

❷ Keep going until you reach the coastguard station at Hall Road. The stone wall at the end of the promenade is a favourite place for fishermen at high tide. If you wish you can cut the walk short here and walk inland along Hall Road West to Hall Road Station, about half a kilometre away. Alternatively you can take the little path from the car park.

❸ To continue, remain with the shore beyond the end of the promenade, going along the path. Between the two beached lightships is a good place to look for wading birds such as oystercatchers, redshank and dunlin.

❹ Just past the second lightship bear right at the waymark along a path through the low sandhills. This winds through growths of creeping willow, tough grasses and stands of sea buckthorn. Turn left where the path forks by a post. Follow the white-topped posts to reach the sailing clubhouse. Here a

board points the way to a viewpoint (at low tide) over the remains of an ancient submerged forest.

❺ Rejoin the path through the dunes. Follow the white-topped posts leading to the Alt estuary and a boatyard. Keep an eye out for shore birds, including the curlew and the bar-tailed godwit, in the Alt estuary.

❻ Walk up the path to the road and turn right. Go down the road, cross the roundabout and keep ahead along Lower Alt Road to find Hightown Station.

access information

Take a train to Waterloo Mersey Station. The suggested return is from Hall Road Station for a short walk, or Hightown Station for the longer walk – trains run every 15 minutes.

Liverpool's revitalized 19th-century dockside area now includes shops, restaurants, art galleries and commercial premises.

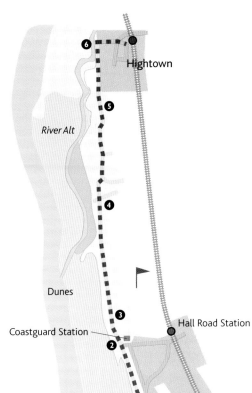

Hightown

River Alt

Dunes

Coastguard Station

Blundellsands

Hall Road Station

Marine Lake

Waterloo

further information

Waterloo to Hall Road is accessible to wheelchair users. For a longer challenge the Sefton Coastal Path links the entire length from Waterloo to Southport, crossing high sandhills and meandering through shady pine woods and rich farmland. It is waymarked throughout by yellow disks with a toad on them. Linking paths lead to all the stations on the Northern Line.

0   1 km   1 mile

▲ Map: Explorer 286
▲ Distance: 14.5 km/9 miles
▲ Walk ID: 732 Jim Grindle

Difficulty rating

Time
●●●●●

▲ Sea, Pub, Toilets, Play Area, Birds, Great Views, Good for Wheelchairs

Blackpool from Fleetwood

This is a linear walk along the Lancashire coast, from Fleetwood to the Pleasure Beach in Blackpool. By keeping to the beach where possible, and using the lower levels of the walks along the sea defences, you can keep well away from traffic.

❶ Cross the road from the North Euston Hotel and turn left on the promenade until you reach the pier 200 m away. Continue for another 50 m past the pier until you come to a turning on the right, beside a notice board, which brings you to the sea wall. Keeping to the beach or the embankment, turn and follow the promenade as it curves to the left. Simply continue south, with the sea to your right, until you reach Cleveleys.

❷ Continue on the promenade until the path curves up to the left to meet the main road. Continue to head south along the road.

❸ At Little Bispham you can turn left if you prefer to catch a tram back to Fleetwood, or you can carry on south to Blackpool (you may have to walk

access information

You can take a train to Blackpool and then a tram to the terminus in Fleetwood. By road it is easiest to come by the M6 to junction 32; the M55 to junction 3 and then the A585 to Fleetwood. There is free parking near the North Euston Hotel which is right on the sea front at the very north of Fleetwood.

along the upper promenade for part of the way if restoration work is taking place). Carry straight on along the promenade until you reach Blackpool's North Pier.

❹ If you wish to extend the walk, it is 3.5 km from here, past the South Pier, to the Pleasure Beach at Blackpool. You can then take a tram back to Fleetwood.

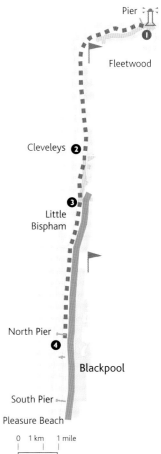

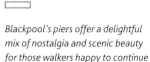

Blackpool's piers offer a delightful mix of nostalgia and scenic beauty for those walkers happy to continue to the end of this route.

▲ Map: Explorer 285
▲ Distance: 6 km/3¾ miles
▲ Walk ID: 257 Jim Grindle

Difficulty rating

Time

▲ Sea, Pub, Toilets, National Trust/NTS,
Wildlife, Birds, Flowers, Great Views,
Good for Wheelchairs

Fisherman's Path from Freshfield

This walk follows the railway line and enters pine woods before reaching the shore.
Views from the beach take in the North Wales Clwydian Hills and the Carneddau.
In clear conditions you can see the Lake District.

❶ On leaving the station turn left and
left again at the telephone box. Walk
past a row of shops and then the station
car park. At the end of the car park
continue on the road which becomes a
gravelled track. Take the wide left fork
following the railway line as far as the
level crossing.

❷ Go over the railway line and follow
the track through a golf course until you
reach a metal gate at the entrance to
the National Nature Reserve.

❸ Take the left fork, which takes you for
1 km between the golf course on the left
and the nature reserve on the right. Go
through a more open area and you reach
a junction by the sand dunes.

❹ Take the fork left, which has woods to
the left and the sea behind the dunes to
the right. After 1 km the path leads to
the beach. Walk along the beach. The
paths going off the beach are marked by
posts. Continue as far as the fourth post,
marked Victoria Road South, then turn
left and climb by the fence to the top of
the dunes.

❺ A boardwalk leads down into
the car park. Keep going until
you reach a road leading to the
Wardens' hut. Look on the right
for 'Squirrel Walk' – this is the
best place to see red squirrels.

❻ Keep straight on and the
concrete road gives way to tarmac –
Victoria Road. It is now less than
1 km back to the station directly
down this road.

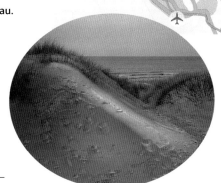

*The hills of North Wales can be viewed
from the sand dunes of Formby Point.*

access information

The walk starts at Freshfield Station on the
Southport/Liverpool line. Access by road is
from the A565. Follow the tourist signs to
Formby Point (National Trust). The route
crosses the railway line where there is
parking.

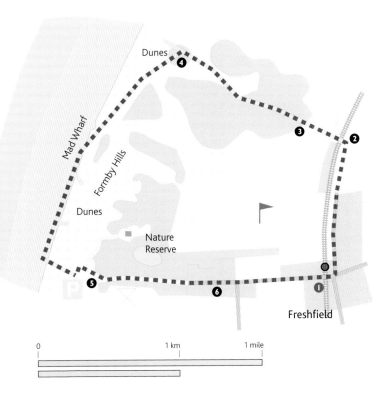

▲ Map: Explorer OL 7

▲ Distance: 11 km/6¾ miles

▲ Walk ID: 919 William Kembery

Difficulty rating

Time

▲ River, Sea, Pub, Toilets, National Trust/NTS, Wildlife, Birds, Flowers, Great Views, Food Shop, Good for Kids, Moor, Tea Shop, Woodland

Leighton Moss and Jenny Brown's Point

This is a varied walk that will take you through woods and along quiet lanes. The walk includes a stretch of Morecambe Bay's rich shores, and passes Leighton Moss bird sanctuary.

1 From the car park take the little gate into Eave's Wood. At the first T-junction turn left. Soon take the right-hand fork going uphill through the trees. At the next junction keep straight on, swinging slightly left.

2 Turn left off the track, but do not go through the gate. Turn right with a stone wall on the left and a hedge on the right. You will arrive at a lane by a bench and a signpost pointing right to Arnside Tower. Cross straight over, along a little lane opposite signed to Cove Road. Follow the narrow lane when it divides, towards a little gate to the left of a house.

3 Go through the gate and onto the lane. Go straight on, to pick up the footpath again. Above Cove Road turn right and, when the footpath ends, cross the road and take the footpath on the other side. As it swings right, take the little road off to the left, signposted to the shore. Go through the gate and turn left along the shore, keeping near the base of the cliffs.

4 After about 1 km, take a little road leading up from the shore. Go through the gate stile to follow the road. Soon take a right-hand footpath, signposted Lindeth Road. At the road, turn right and follow it until it forks with Hollins Lane going off to the left.

5 Take the right-hand fork signed Jenny Brown's Point. Look out for a little gate on the right. Go through the gate and follow the good footpath across the heathland round to the left, parallel to the wall. Follow the footpath down into the bay. Continue with the footpath through the trees. Soon pass through two kissing gates. Turn right along the road. Just before Jenny Brown's Houses take the little causeway down onto the shore and past the old smelt chimney. Follow the base of the cliffs to a stile.

6 Go through and continue with the fence on the right. At a metal gate go straight on. The footpath slopes gently uphill into the woods from a solid stone stile. At the road turn right and at the first junction turn right again. At the next major junction keep straight on towards the station. Soon a little lane goes off to the left. Take this lane to return to the car park.

access information

Silverdale is west of the M6, north of Morecambe Bay. Begin the walk at Eave's Wood car park, north of Silverdale train station. If arriving by public transport, there is a regular train service from Lancaster or Carlisle.

The extensive tidal flats of Morecambe Bay are one of the most important bird reserves in Britain.

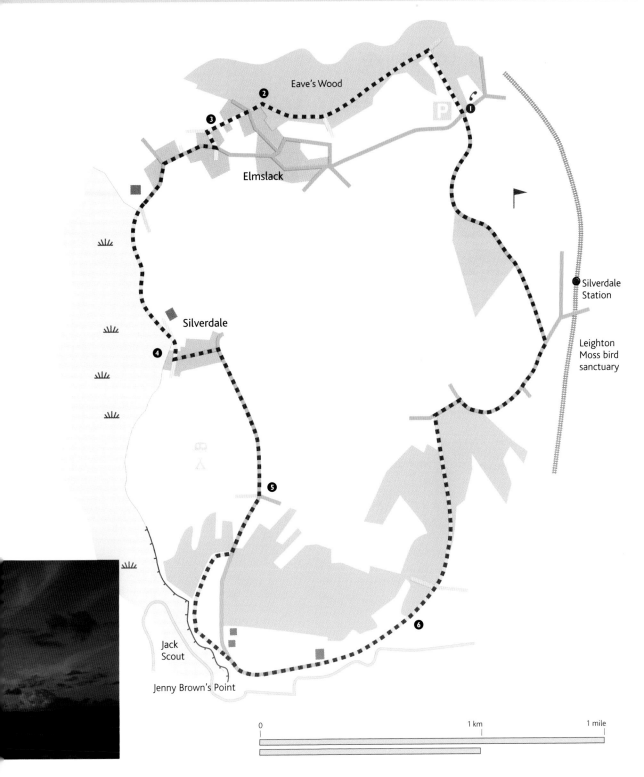

Eave's Wood

❷

❸

Elmslack

Silverdale

❹

Silverdale
Station

Leighton
Moss bird
sanctuary

P

❶

❺

Jack
Scout

Jenny Brown's Point

❻

0   1 km   1 mile

▲ Map: Explorer OL 7

▲ Distance: 6 km/3¾ miles

▲ Walk ID: 1299 Gary Gray

Difficulty rating

👣 👣

Time

● ● ◗

▲ Lake/Loch, Pub, National Trust/NTS, Wildlife, Birds, Flowers, Great Views

Black Crag from Tarn Hows

This is a very pleasant, easy-to-follow, linear walk along Tarn Hows and up to Black Crag. The fantastic views include a panorama of nearly all the major fells.

❶ From the car park walk out onto the road. The path down to the tarn is straight ahead. Take the right-hand fork towards the tarn. On reaching the gate, go through and follow the path alongside the tarn.

❷ At the signpost (Arnside and Langdale), turn left. This is part of the Cumbrian Way. This track leads you away from the tarn. On reaching a gate and stile, turn right onto a stone track. There are fine views of Tarn Hows to the right about two-thirds of the way up.

❸ When you reach the plantation of Iron Keld on your left, look for a gate and a signpost marked 'Iron Keld'. Turn left through the gate and follow the track through the plantation.

❹ As you emerge from the plantation, you will reach a gate and swing gate. Go through and walk on for a short way through an old set of stone gateposts. A path joins from the right at a sharp angle. Take this path which first doubles back then soon swings up to the left and towards the fell. Follow the grassy track upwards.

❺ On reaching the summit there is a trig point at the top. You can continue over the stile and along the fell. However, there is no way down and you must return to the stile and the track. For your return journey, simply head back the way you came.

Tarn Hows is a man-made landscaped pool, surrounded by woodland.

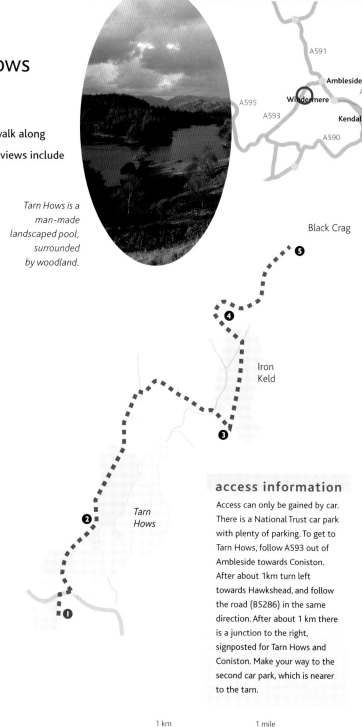

Black Crag

Iron Keld

Tarn Hows

access information

Access can only be gained by car. There is a National Trust car park with plenty of parking. To get to Tarn Hows, follow A593 out of Ambleside towards Coniston. After about 1km turn left towards Hawkshead, and follow the road (B5286) in the same direction. After about 1 km there is a junction to the right, signposted for Tarn Hows and Coniston. Make your way to the second car park, which is nearer to the tarn.

0   1 km   1 mile

▲ Map: Explorer OL 4
▲ Distance: 6 km/3¾ miles
▲ Walk ID: 173 David Stewart

Difficulty rating

Time

▲ Hills or Fells, Lake/Loch, Pub, Toilets, Church, National Trust/NTS, Birds, Great Views

Buttermere

A charming walk that takes you on a circuit of Buttermere, one of the prettiest and most isolated of the lakes. The mere itself nestles at the end of its valley, with the steep sides of Red Pike, High Stile and High Crag rising up directly from it.

❶ Pass down to the left of the Fish Inn and head for the lake. Immediately, you can see the waters of Sour Milk Gill cascading down the hillside. Head towards the waterfall, ignoring the path signed to Scale Force on your right.

❷ As you reach the lake edge bear right and make straight for the base of the fall. From here it is a truly impressive sight, especially after a good rainfall. Turn left to follow the lakeside, taking the path that runs right by the water's edge. It is very difficult to go wrong, so all you need do is soak up the glorious scenery.

❸ After a kilometre or so, the path runs beyond the end of the lake, and you will see a track to the left passing over Peggy's Bridge in the direction of Gatesgarth Farm. Follow the track, taking time to stop at the bridge, where you can admire the spectacular view along the lake. Continue up to the farm.

❹ Turn left onto the road. There is a short stretch of tarmac here, but it is a quiet route. Shortly you come to a small bay and the lakeside path forks away from the road. The path follows closely along the lake edge.

❺ Before you reach the village again, pass through a short tunnel hewn into the rock (mind your head, as the sign here warns!).

❻ Once you get beyond the lake, follow the well-signed paths back to the village.

access information

By car, take the B5289 from Keswick. From Cockermouth take the B5292, then the B5289. There are regular services by bus from Keswick and Cockermouth during the daytime.

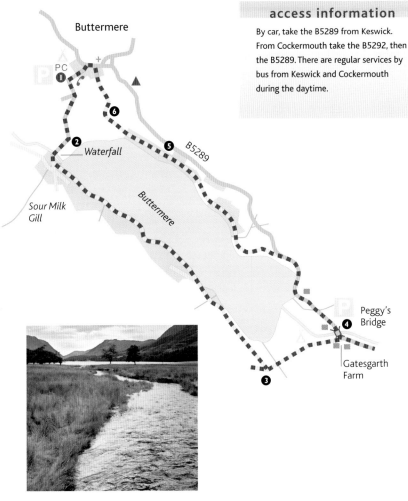

Buttermere nestles at the end of a steep-sided valley, surrounded by the peaks of Red Pike, High Stile and High Crag.

▲ Map: Explorer OL 7
▲ Distance: 11¼ km/7 miles
▲ Walk ID: 1268 Harold Toze

Difficulty rating

‼‼‼

Time

●●●●

▲ Hills or Fells, River, Lake/Loch, Pub, Toilets, Wildlife, Great Views, Gift Shop, Industrial Archaeology, Tea Shop, Waterfall, Woodland

Skelwith Bridge from Elterwater

This is a low-level walk with many interesting features to look out for along the way, including two waterfalls – Colwith Force and Skelwith Force – and an old clapper bridge at Slater Bridge.

❶ From the car park entrance turn left to cross the bridge. Go along the road and take the lane that forks off to the right. Continue on the rough track. Go over the hill and down to the minor road through Little Langdale.

❷ At the road junction cross diagonally down a farm track. At the farm buildings follow the footpath alongside the stone wall. Cross Slater Bridge and go up the track on the other side through a stile onto a wider track. Turn left and follow the stream. Go along the track ahead to the next footbridge/ford.

❸ Follow the track away from the ford up the slope to the right. Follow the left fork signposted Skelwith and Colwith. Continue uphill to Stang End and along the road to High Park Farm. After the farm take the path leading off to the left. Go across the field and through a gate. Follow a small footpath downhill to arrive at Colwith Force waterfall. Continue alongside the stream to come out on a minor road. Turn right and after about 100 m there is a footpath signposted to Skelwith Bridge.

❹ Turn left onto the footpath. At Park Farm take the right-hand path to the bridge. The path continues parallel to the road, eventually joining it. Continue down the main road to Skelwith Bridge. At the bottom of the hill turn left, crossing the river by the road bridge.

Skelwith Force is a short distance up the stream. Pass by the Skelwith Bridge Hotel to the junction of the B5343 and the A593. Cross the B5343 coming from the left and go up the minor road. At the top of the hill turn right along the Ambleside road, then almost immediately left on a minor road. Turn right again at another minor road, which is marked to Loughrigg Tarn only.

❺ Pass Dillygarth Cottage and turn left along a rough track. Follow the track around the north side of Loughrigg Tarn. At the Howe turn left through a wooden gate and down the hill to pass near to the end of Loughrigg Tarn. At the minor road turn left. Soon a track leads off to the right, signed back to Skelwith Bridge. Take this track, passing Crag Head Cottage on the left. Just before the dry-stone wall turn right and at the top of the next rise Elterwater should come into view through the trees. Continue downhill and go through a stile in the stone wall into the wood beyond. You will reach Langdale Road.

❻ Cross Langdale Road diagonally and hop over the low wall alongside the wooden gate. Follow the track down the slope to join the main track beside Elterwater and continue along this track to return to the car park.

access information

Elterwater is on the B5343 to the west of Ambleside. There are two car parks in Elterwater. This walk starts from the lower car park.

The peaks of the spectacular Langdale Valley, which include Pavey Ark, Pike o'Stickle and Bow Fell, are a popular destination for hillwalkers.

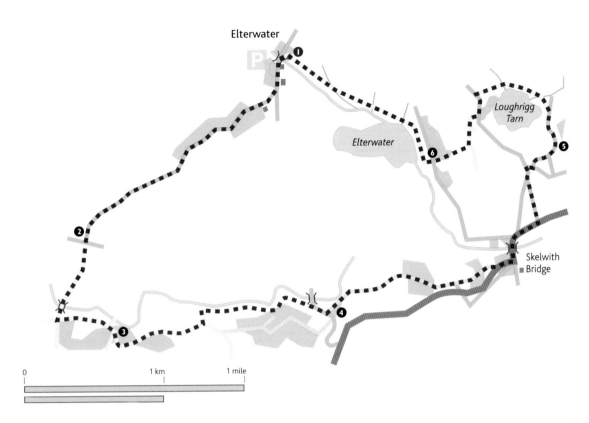

Elterwater

Loughrigg
Tarn

Elterwater

Skelwith
Bridge

0   1 km   1 mile

Woodland & Hillside

From picturesque woods to the dramatic fells of the Lake District, the woodland and hillside walks in this region are simply breathtaking. Highlights include the Sandstone Trail and Dungeon Ghyll.

▲ Map: Explorer 19
▲ Distance: 10 km/6¼ miles
▲ Walk ID: 786 Barry Smith

Difficulty rating

Time

▲ River, Pub, Toilets, Wildlife, Woodland, Flowers, Good for Wheelchairs

Tockholes Plantations from Abbey Village

A delightful walk that includes a lovely valley, with some breathtaking views at the start, then enters steep woodland, which includes the Tockholes Plantations. There are bluebells in the spring and early summer, wild garlic, fungi and native trees.

1 From the corner of the car park, go through the gateposts towards the reservoir. Ignore the stile to the farm on the left. Turn left at the footpath sign next to a house. Follow the track and cross the water run-off, using the bridge if the water is running. Follow the track to the embankment of Roddlesworth Reservoir. Go left at the concrete 'seats'.

2 At the other end of the embankment, bear right to enter the woodland. At the next signpost, bear slightly right to go downhill with the path to a gate and stile at the next embankment. Go left with the smaller path.

3 Keeping to the path by the wall and the reservoir, rejoin the main path and turn right. At the next junction, signed for the Visitor Centre, keep straight on and the same at the next, to go downhill once again and come out at a gate and bridge at the River Roddlesworth.

4 Turn right. Cross the bridge and go through the kissing gate in the wall. Follow the track by the river, in the most delightful part of the walk, over a small bridge and up and down steps, until you come to a fence and bridge where you bear left on a wider track through woods.

5 Go over a stile and continue straight on to the junction and bear right with the smaller footpath sign, to continue through woodland. When you reach a wall and gap, cross the footbridge and bear left again with the smaller footpath sign, on the path next to the reservoir.

6 Turn right at the footbridge to come to the concrete seats once again. Turn left and follow the footpath back to the car park at the start.

further information

If you wish to include a visit to Hollinshead Hall it will extend this walk by 2.5 km, but it is well worth the effort. Make the hall your first port of call if you start at Slipper Lowe car park or the Visitor Centre at Tockholes.

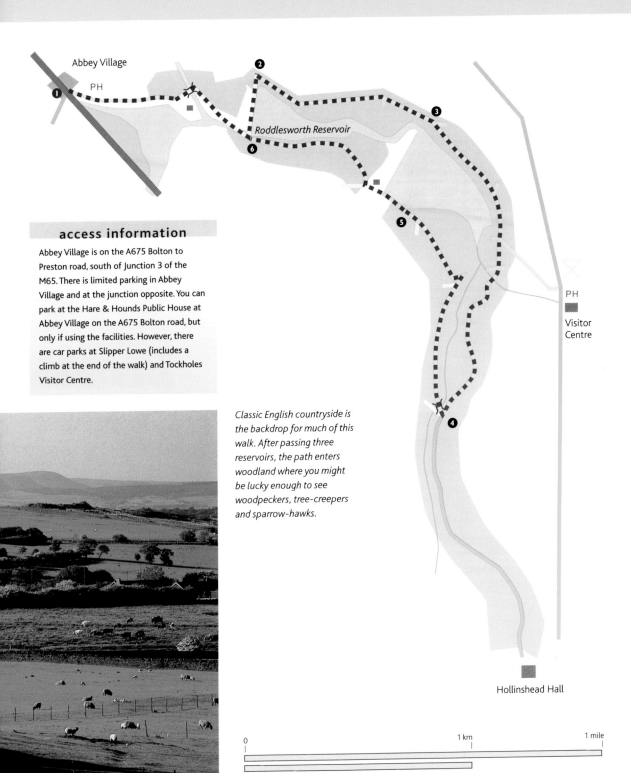

Abbey Village

PH

1

2

6

Roddlesworth Reservoir

3

5

4

PH

Visitor
Centre

Hollinshead Hall

access information

Abbey Village is on the A675 Bolton to Preston road, south of Junction 3 of the M65. There is limited parking in Abbey Village and at the junction opposite. You can park at the Hare & Hounds Public House at Abbey Village on the A675 Bolton road, but only if using the facilities. However, there are car parks at Slipper Lowe (includes a climb at the end of the walk) and Tockholes Visitor Centre.

Classic English countryside is the backdrop for much of this walk. After passing three reservoirs, the path enters woodland where you might be lucky enough to see woodpeckers, tree-creepers and sparrow-hawks.

0   1 km   1 mile

▲ Map: Explorer 267
▲ Distance: 6 km/3¾ miles
▲ Walk ID: 234 R. & C. Jones

Difficulty rating

Time

▲ Toilets, Wildlife, Birds, Flowers, Great Views

The Sandstone Trail from Delamere

This walk starts from Delamere Station and follows country roads and the Sandstone Trail within the Delamere Forest. The Sandstone Trail runs from Frodsham in the north to Grindley Brook on the Shropshire border.

1 Leave the car park and walk towards the railway station entrance. In front of the station turn right and head for the main road. On reaching the main road turn right and walk along the footpath on the other side of the road for about a kilometre. There are good views to the left on a clear day. To the right is a hill on which was once a Saxon hill fort.

2 On reaching the road junction with Eddisbury Hill turn right, and climb the hill. Continue along this road until you reach the junction with Stoney Lane.

3 Cross over onto a sandy track and follow the path. You are now on the course of an old Roman road. On reaching the gate cross the stile and enter a large field. Keep straight ahead keeping the field boundary on your right, and head for the far right-hand corner of the field. Cross the stile and continue along a path bounded by trees. Cross this stile and enter Nettleford Wood.

4 On reaching the crossing path turn right on the Sandstone Trail. When you get to the footpath sign keep straight ahead, and cross the stile next to the five-barred gate. Follow the grassy track, which eventually starts to descend.

5 On reaching the junction with Eddisbury Lodge in front of you, turn right along the road. This will lead you past the Delamere Visitor Centre.

6 Just past the Visitor Centre is a bridge over the railway. At the side of the bridge is an alleyway, which leads back down to the car park.

access information

This walk starts at Delamere Railway Station. Access by car is via the A556 and then the B5152, which leads to the Lindmere Picnic site adjacent to the station.

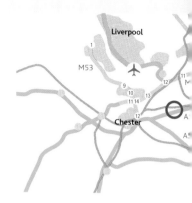

A stirring view of Shropshire's beautiful pine forests.

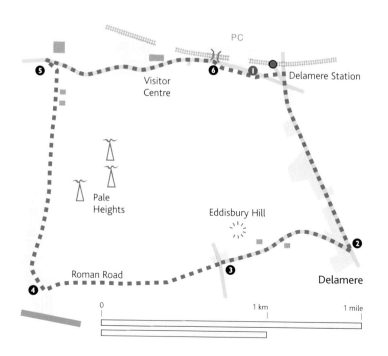

▲ Map: Explorer 285
▲ Distance: 4 km/2½ miles
▲ Walk ID: 255 Jim Grindle

Difficulty rating

Time

▲ Pub, National Trust/NTS, Wildlife

Southport

Formby

Liverpool

M6

A59
A565

M58

M57

A580

M62

Wigan

Freshfield and Dobson's Ride

Although this footpath is on the coast, we have classified it as a woodland walk because it is a very quick and easy stroll through tranquil Corsican pine woods. You may be lucky enough to see some of the area's red squirrels.

❶ On leaving Freshfield Station turn left, and left again at the telephone box. Walk past the row of shops and then the station car park. At the end of the car park you can continue on the road or branch left onto the bridleway – they join up again further on. The tarmac ends at the last house and becomes a gravelled track.

❷ Take the fork left on the wider track following the railway line as far as a level crossing. Go over the railway line and follow the track through a golf course until you reach a metal gate at the entrance to the National Nature Reserve.

❸ Take the right fork, passing round the end of the golf course on a winding track until you reach a junction.

❹ Go left at this junction, following the signpost for the Sefton Coastal Footpath. After 100 m the sandy path turns right by a white-topped post and after another 50 m it enters the wood. Do not go through the gate on the left – it is 'No Entry'. The track winds through the

wood for 1 km with white-topped posts to keep you on the right route. At the end of the wood you come to a broad, stony track – Dobson's Ride.

❺ Turn right and follow the track for a further kilometre, crossing an open area and then entering the wood again. The path drops a little and you come to a fork with a white post.

❻ Stay on the main track by turning left at the white post. In 50 m you will come back to the path to retrace your steps on the outward route.

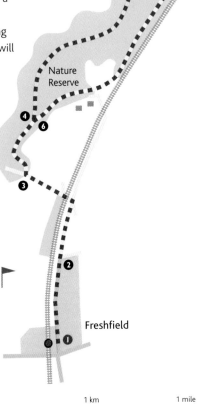

Nature Reserve

Freshfield

This is one of the few areas of Britain where you may be able to see the native red squirrel, now an endangered species.

access information

The walk starts at Freshfield Station on the Southport/Liverpool line. Access by road is from the A565. Follow the tourist signs to Formby Point (National Trust). The route crosses the railway line at Freshfield Station where there is parking.

0   1 km   1 mile

▲ Map: Explorer OL 6
▲ Distance: 10 km/6¼ miles
▲ Walk ID: 378 Samantha Asher

Difficulty rating

Time

▲ Hills or Fells, Pub, Toilets, Museum, Play Area, Castle, National Trust/NTS, Wildlife, Birds, Great Views

Eskdale Green to Muncaster Head

Take a walk from Eskdale Green to Muncaster Fell, stopping at Muncaster Castle if desired. The return journey, via a bridleway, cuts through a forest to Muncaster Head and back to Eskdale Green.

❶ Proceed down the road named Randlehow, which is opposite the post office. At the T-junction, turn right. Go through the wooden gate beside the cattle grid. Proceed to a gap in the dry-stone wall on your right, marked 'footpath'.

❷ Go through the gap. Follow the path across the field to a kissing gate beside the railway line. Pass through the kissing gate, cross the railway line and go through another kissing gate. Continue ahead. Cross a small stream and a kissing gate. Follow the right-hand perimeter of the field, until you reach a crossing track at its other side.

❸ Turn left. Look for two arrows on a wooden post. (If you reach a stile beside a metal farm gate, you have gone too far.) Turn right up Muncaster Fell in the direction of the arrows. Continue uphill to a wooden gate beside a kissing gate. Go through it and climb the path over Muncaster Fell.

❹ Pass through a gap in a dry-stone wall. Continue straight ahead. As you proceed, a triangulation point can be seen ahead and to your right. The River Esk is visible ahead where it meets the Irish Sea at Ravenglass, and to the right is Sellafield Nuclear Power Plant.

❺ Keeping the triangulation point to your right, continue downhill to a forest. With the forest on your right, proceed to a kissing gate beside a wooden gate. Pass through and continue ahead on a track which runs between rhododendron bushes. Muncaster Tarn is visible to your right. Follow the track downhill to a track off to the left (signposted to Lower Eskdale) and a sign straight on to Muncaster.

further information

The triangulation point marks the highest point of Muncaster Fell at 231 m above sea level.

Dry-stone walls crisscross the fells above Eskdale.

⑥ If you wish to make a detour to Muncaster Castle, go straight ahead instead of turning left. Otherwise, turn left and follow the path through woodland to a metal gate. Go through the gap to the left of the gate and continue downhill past a turning on the left and a house on the right, behind which you will see a monument. The path joins a tarmac road. Continue straight ahead past some houses.

⑦ Immediately after the last house, the tarmac road becomes a track. Pass through a wooden gate and continue ahead on the track for approx 2.5 km.

Look out for the Roman Tile Kilns, Cropple How plantation and Brantrake Crags (259 m) to the right of the track. Proceed to Muncaster Head farmhouse.

⑧ Go through a metal gate. Proceed down the track as it bends left just before the farmhouse and continue uphill between farm buildings on your right and a dry-stone wall on your left. Follow the track through a wooden gate beside a metal gate. Pass over a stile beside another metal gate. Proceed, following arrows on a wooden post, ignoring a path off to your left, back to Eskdale Post Office.

access information

Take the railway to Ravenglass and then take the narrow-gauge 'Ravenglass and Eskdale' railway to 'The Green' Station, walk uphill (i.e. away from the pub) to start the walk opposite the post office. By car, parking is available some 50 m before and after the post office.

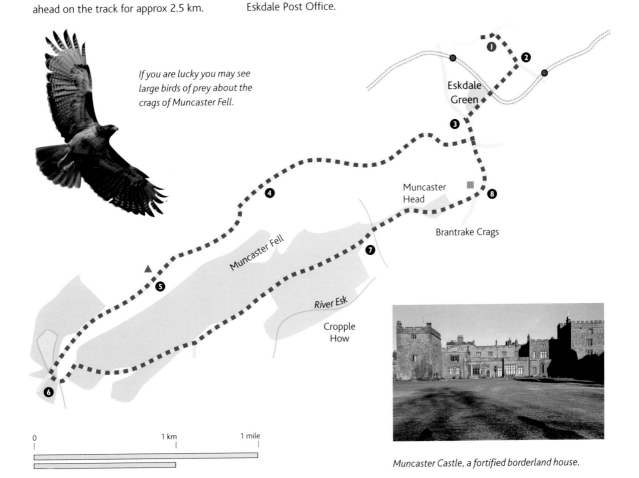

If you are lucky you may see large birds of prey about the crags of Muncaster Fell.

Eskdale Green

Muncaster Head

Brantrake Crags

Muncaster Fell

River Esk

Cropple How

0   1 km   1 mile

Muncaster Castle, a fortified borderland house.

▲ Map: Explorer OL 7

▲ Distance: 6 km/3¾ miles

▲ Walk ID: 1390 Jim Grindle

Difficulty rating

Time

▲ Hills or Fells, River, Lake/Loch, Toilets, Museum, Church, National Trust/NTS, Wildlife, Flowers, Great Views, Food Shop, Tea Shop

Alcock Tarn from Grasmere

In this walk a lane gives way to a track rising gradually above the Vale of Grasmere. The tarn itself is an attractive, quiet spot. The return is across beautiful meadows.

❶ Turn right as you leave the Information Centre and walk up to the junction by the church. Turn right and go past the main car park to the junction with the main road. Turn left to the new crossing point. Go over and turn right. A lane branches off from the main road. Follow signs for Dove Cottage.

❷ Take the left fork along the lane. At the top the lane forks again. Take the left fork and then watch for a track on the left signposted to Alcock Tarn. Where the track splits you will see a little gate.

❸ Go through the gate onto the track that leads up to the tarn. Go left of the tarn to a stile in the wall at the far end. Beyond the wall the track leads down to a beck. Cross the bridge and go through the gate onto a drive. This drops to a junction with a lane.

❹ Turn left to come to another lane on the left. Turn and follow the lane down to the main road. Just to the right on the main road is a crossing point. Go over and turn left to reach a gate 50 m away.

❺ Go along the enclosed track into the field at the end and then follow the right field edge to the first of a sequence of gates. You will reach a newly built bridge. Cross the bridge and turn left.

❻ This path will bring you out at the church in the centre of the village. Turn left and take the first turning on the right for the Information Centre.

access information

Grasmere is north of Ambleside on the A591 Ambleside/Keswick road. There are three large car parks in the village and some smaller ones. Buses from Ambleside to Keswick call in at the village.

A picturesque bridge across a lakeland beck is a good place to admire the views after visiting Alcock Tarn.

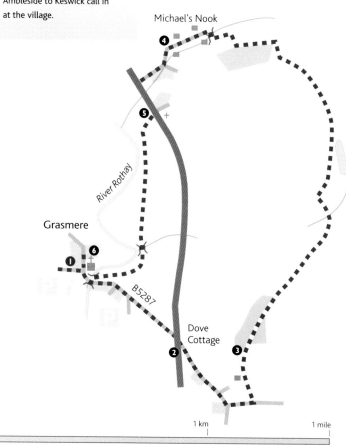

▲ Map: Explorer OL 6 & 7
▲ Distance: 10 km/6¼ miles
▲ Walk ID: 341 Jude Howat

Difficulty rating

Time

▲ River, Pub, Wildlife, Great Views

Dungeon Ghyll from Elterwater

This scenic low-level walk follows the course of the Langdale Beck up to Dungeon Ghyll, then returns part way up the side of the valley through some forestry to Elterwater.

1 From the car park, turn left and cross the bridge to the start of the walk. After crossing the bridge, take the road to the right at the T-junction. Follow the track until you reach a mine entrance in the rock face. Opposite this is a footpath heading down the hill towards the beck. Take this path and follow it over a footbridge.

2 You will come out into a car park in the village of Chapel Stile. Walk along the road for about 100 m and take the next footpath to the left. Follow this up a small hill. Continue straight on, keeping on the path just to the right of the white buildings.

3 Keep left. Soon you will cross a bridge over the beck. The path bends to the right. Continue along the track close to the water's edge. Cross the beck again at the bridge. Follow the path up to the main road.

4 Pass through the swing gate and turn left. Walk along the road for about 100 m, then turn left onto the track. Follow it until you rejoin the main road. Turn left and walk along it for 200 m.

5 Turn left onto the track over the bridge. Cross the field towards a farm house. Keep left. Pass through the swing gate, then cross the small bridge and turn left onto the path. Turn right by the disused barn. Follow the path over the hill, heading eastwards.

6 Continue straight on, following the main path all the way until you reach a road. Turn left and follow the road. Turn left again. This road will take you back down to the starting point by the bridge.

access information

Elterwater is on the B5343 to the north-west of Ambleside close to the lovely valley of Langdale. There is pay-and-display parking in Elterwater, where this walk starts, but you can start in Dungeon Ghyll, where pay-and-display parking is also available.

A breathtaking overview of Langdale, showing the course of Great Langdale Beck.

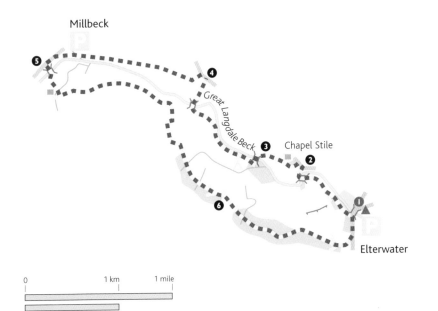

▲ Map: Explorer OL 7

▲ Distance: 8 km/5 miles

▲ Walk ID: 1340 Gary Gray

Difficulty rating

Time

▲ Pub, Toilets, National Trust/NTS, Wildlife, Great Views, Café, Food Shop, Good for Kids, Public Transport, Nature Trail, Tea Shop, Woodland

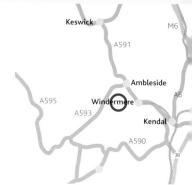

Latterbarrow from Hawkshead

A walk across open fields is followed by a short climb to the summit of Latterbarrow with its tall cairn visible from Hawkshead. The stroll back is through pleasant forest.

1 Starting from the Red Lion Pub in Hawkshead village, follow the path that runs down the side of the pub to the main road. Go across the road and down another path. The path dog-legs right and then left, and eventually leads to a small footbridge.

2 Turn left and walk alongside the fence to the corner of the field. Turn right and walk to the far corner where there is a kissing gate. Go through the gate and walk diagonally right across the field. Go through another kissing gate and turn left. There is a signpost for Loanthwaite. The path goes through two further fields and over two stiles. After the second stile follow the path right across the field up to a gate.

3 Go through the gate and left onto a track towards a large oak tree, which is on the right side of the track. Go over the stile next to the tree and follow the path. There is a fence on your right. Go through the gate and continue on the path, with the fence now on your left side.

Hawkshead offers fantastic views, not least from the summit of Latterbarrow, which looms over the village.

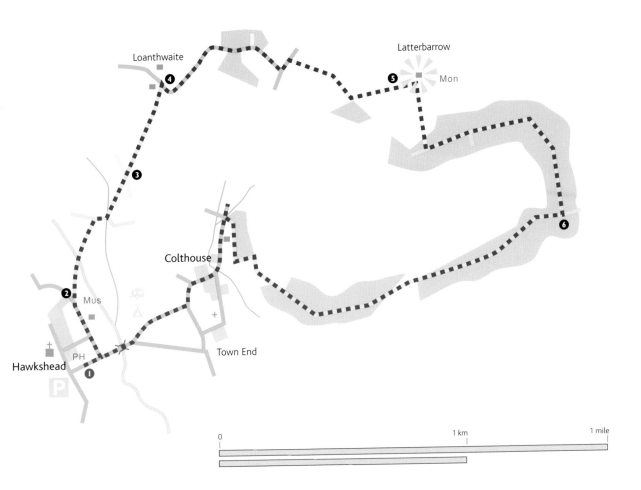

4 The path leads to the right of a farm. At the minor road (Loanthwaite Lane) turn right and follow it to a T-junction. Turn left onto this road and walk on for a short distance. On the right side of the road is a gate signposted Latterbarrow. Go through the gate and follow the track up through the trees. Follow the stone wall to your right and a grassy track to the left leads to the summit.

5 On reaching the summit, you will find the monument and good views. At the monument, go right. The grassy path leads you downhill to a corner and a stone wall and stile. Go left over the stile and follow the path into the forest. The path goes down a steep embankment. Keep to the well-defined main path.

6 The path reaches a gate in a wall, by a T-junction. Go through the gate onto a hard track and follow the signs for Hawkshead. The path leads to a road. Go left and follow the road towards Town End. Turn right at the T-junction and walk along the minor road back to the start at Hawkshead.

access information

The walk starts in Hawkshead, on the B5285 south of Ambleside. There are several large car parks, which are pay-and-display. These get busy at peak holiday times.

WOODLAND & HILLSIDE **87**

Wales

Coastal & Waterside

From glorious coastlines, to dramatic waterfalls and quiet canals, Wales has so much to offer the walker in search of waterside tranquillity. Highlights include the Devil's Kitchen and Colwyn Bay.

▲ Map: Explorer 255 or 256
▲ Distance: 10.6 km/6½ miles
▲ Walk ID: 312 Jim Grindle

Difficulty rating

Time

▲ Hills or Fells, River, Pub, Toilets, Museum, Castle, Stately Home, Birds, Flowers, Great Views

Llangollen Canal Walk

A walk along the canal with a return by bridleway, which snakes round the hillside offering outstanding views. The walk includes a climb to the top of Dinas Bran, the ancient castle overlooking the town of LLangollen.

❶ Turn right from the car park entrance and walk to the main street. Turn left. Cross the bridge and go half-left across the main road to a passageway with a signpost for canal boats. Go up the narrow path or steps. On the towpath turn right and go under the road bridge. Follow the towpath for 2 km to reach another bridge.

❷ Cross the stile by the gate and turn left on the lane, crossing the canal bridge. Go uphill until you reach Llandyn Hall. On the left is a stile. Go over and up to another stile by a gate 200 m away. Cross the two stiles near to each other. Go half-left across the field. Go through the gate and follow the hedge and then the buildings on the left until you reach a stile onto a lane. Turn right. You will reach a kissing gate and signpost for the castle.

❸ Follow the signpost pointing left. Go over the stile at the end of the path and turn left. Go straight uphill to the castle. On the far side you will be able to pick up a broad, fenced track leading down. Turn right at the second tree. Continue until you reach a fence. Turn left and go down towards a stile. Cross the field to the far right corner to a stile by a lane.

❹ Turn right and stay on the lane for 500 m. Turn right at the junction and look for the signpost for Brynhyfryd.

Turn left and pass a building close on your left and two others up to the right. Go through a gate and onto a grassy track for 1.2 km, after which it drops and joins another. Turn left so that you double back. After 120 m you come to a ladder stile on the right. Cross and look for another one in the corner. Go over and follow the field edge.

❺ Follow the sign towards Llangollen. You soon come to a gate. Follow an enclosed track to a road. Turn right. You come to a canal bridge on the left.

❻ Cross the bridge, turn left and follow the towpath for 2 km back to Llangollen.

access information

Llangollen is just off the A5 and is signposted from the A483. There is a car park in the centre of town, again well signposted. There are regular buses to Chester, Chirk, Wrexham and Oswestry.

The Offa's Dyke Path, which runs along the hills above Llangollen, traces the border built between England and Wales in 770, when Wales effectively became a separate Celtic nation.

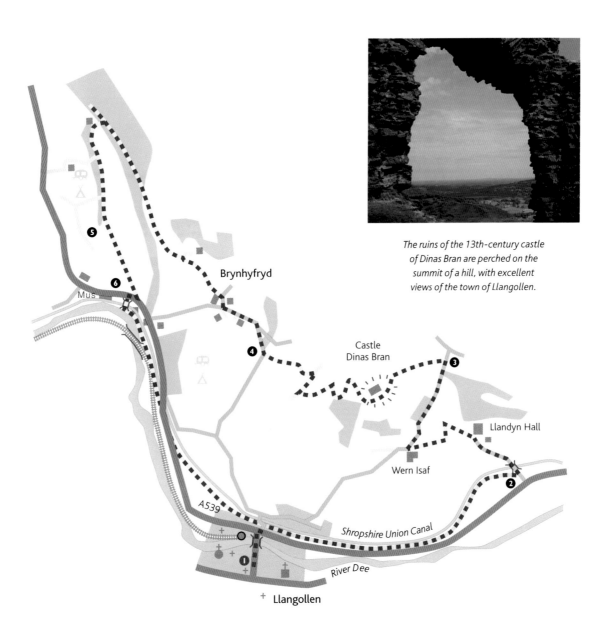

The ruins of the 13th-century castle of Dinas Bran are perched on the summit of a hill, with excellent views of the town of Llangollen.

5

6

Mus

Brynhyfryd

4

Castle
Dinas Bran

3

Llandyn Hall

Wern Isaf

2

A539

Shropshire Union Canal

1

River Dee

Llangollen

0   1 km   1 mile

▲ Map: Explorer OL 23

▲ Distance: 8 km/5 miles

▲ Walk ID: 604 Chris Dixon

Difficulty rating

Time

▲ Mountains, River, Pub, Birds,
Good for Wheelchairs

Mawddach Estuary from Penmaenpool

Following the route of a dismantled railway towards the sea, this walk takes in splendid views of the hilly countryside. The estuary at Barmouth Bridge is a haven for waders and other waterbirds. Parts of the walk pass unspoilt ancient woodland.

1 At the car park you will see a hut and the toll bridge behind it at the start of the walk. From here, head downstream without crossing the river.

2 Just over a small road is a hotel, converted from the old Penmaenpool railway station. The remainder of this walk is along the course of the old railway as it heads towards the sea.

3 Pass through the gate, and after a slight bend the path heads for a kilometre straight across the marsh before reaching the estuary itself. After a further kilometre, you will cross a footbridge.

4 About 2 km later, you may start to get views of the distant Barmouth Bridge, which spans the estuary.

5 You can choose to take the road leading to Morfa Mawddach Station (formerly Barmouth Junction), or follow the route down the track on the right and past a disused platform. If you go to the station, a gate at the end of the one remaining platform links back up with the route.

6 Barmouth Bridge can be crossed for a small toll, but since the tollbooth is at the far side, you can easily go half way for a view out to sea or back up the estuary. From here, retrace your steps to Penmaenpool.

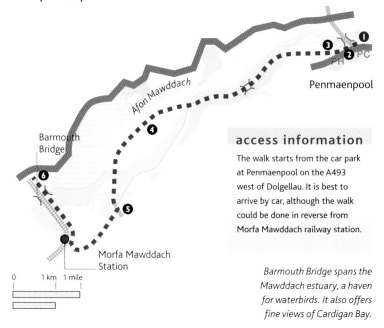

access information

The walk starts from the car park at Penmaenpool on the A493 west of Dolgellau. It is best to arrive by car, although the walk could be done in reverse from Morfa Mawddach railway station.

Barmouth Bridge spans the Mawddach estuary, a haven for waterbirds. It also offers fine views of Cardigan Bay.

▲ Map: Explorer OL 17
▲ Distance: 4.5 km/2¾ miles
▲ Walk ID: 757 Peter Salenieks

Difficulty rating

Time

▲ Mountains, Lake/Loch, Toilets, Great Views

Twll Du (Devil's Kitchen) from Ogwen Cottage

An historic view of the falls at Twll Du (Devil's Kitchen).

A short, scenic circuit of Llyn Idwal from Ogwen Cottage, with views up into Twll Du and across to Pen yr Ole Wen. Ogwen Valley is worth a visit for its splendid glaciated landforms.

❶ The walk starts at the eastern end of the car park. Follow the stone path south, crossing a double stile and then a wooden footbridge. The path bends round to the left, before swinging back to the right after about 200 m. Follow the path to Llyn Idwal, go through a gate and continue along the eastern side of the lake. After passing Idwal Slabs, the path climbs towards the stream.

❷ Cross the stream and continue more steeply along the path until you reach a path junction beside a large boulder.

❸ For a better view into Twll Du, turn left at the large boulder and ascend a little further. When you have finished, continue along the path in front of the large boulder. Turn north and descend towards Llyn Idwal. Stone slabs bridge several small streams as the path goes along the western side of the lake. Bear right along the northern edge of Llyn Idwal, joining the path from Y Garn just before you reach a wooden footbridge.

❹ Cross the footbridge and turn left at the footpath junction, finally rejoining your outward route back to the car park at Ogwen Cottage.

further information

This walk will take about 90 minutes. While it should present few difficulties in good conditions, this is graded as a moderate walk because the stream crossing can be awkward. Under winter conditions, the upper section is deceptively icy and should be attempted only by suitably experienced and equipped walkers.

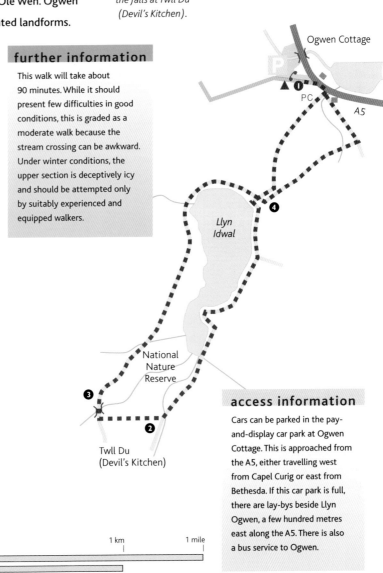

access information

Cars can be parked in the pay-and-display car park at Ogwen Cottage. This is approached from the A5, either travelling west from Capel Curig or east from Bethesda. If this car park is full, there are lay-bys beside Llyn Ogwen, a few hundred metres east along the A5. There is also a bus service to Ogwen.

0   1 km   1 mile

▲ Map: Explorer 264

▲ Distance: 22 km/13¾ miles

▲ Walk ID: 753 Jim Grindle

Difficulty rating

Time

▲ Sea, Pub, Toilets, Church, Great Views

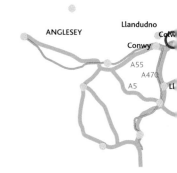

Rhyl from Rhôs-on-Sea

This is an easy-to-follow linear walk along the coast, using a specially made path as well as promenades and sea walls. It goes from west to east to take advantage of the prevailing wind.

Bodnant Castle boasts one of the finest gardens in Britain, famous for its display of rhododendrons, azaleas and magnolias. Perched above the River Conwy valley, the gardens offer fine views of Snowdonia.

❶ Keep Rhôs-on-Sea Information Centre building on your left to begin the walk. After 2 km you approach Colwyn Bay Pier. After another 2 km you have passed Old Colwyn, and the promenade now turns under the railway. A tarmac path branches off on the left. Follow this path.

❷ In 1 km the path rises by sea defence blocks. After another 3 km you cross a bridge. Keep going now for 5 km.

❸ Once you reach the front at Pensarn the railway station of Pensarn and Abergele is only 500 m further on, should you wish to return to Colwyn Bay. The footpath continues between the wall and the railway.

❹ Head towards Rhyl where there is a group of small buildings. Go through the metal kissing gate and onto a red shale path which winds through the dunes. About 300 m away there is a junction with a tarmac path.

❺ Turn right and go through a gate just in front of the bungalows. Go a little to the right to keep in the same direction down Betws Avenue. Turn to the left into Bryn Avenue. At the end of the road turn right and you will reach the Ferry Inn. The main road is just in front. Turn left and make for the bridge over the River Clwyd. Across the river there is a roundabout. Go straight over, following the sign to the railway station, which is still 2 km away. You can walk alongside the Marine Lake for a little. Keep going until you come to the traffic lights by the police station. The railway station is signposted again from here.

❻ From Rhyl you can return to Colwyn Bay by train or taxi.

access information

By car use the A55 Expressway, turning off at the signs for Llandudno and Rhôs-on-Sea. Turn right at the first two sets of traffic lights and right at the first roundabout. Go straight over the next roundabout and turn right at the next lights. This is Rhôs Road which leads directly to a T-junction by the Information Centre.

Views across Colwyn Bay make this a footpath to remember.

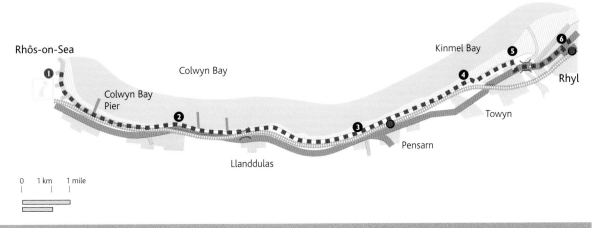

Rhôs-on-Sea

1

Colwyn Bay

Colwyn Bay Pier

2

Llanddulas

3

Pensarn

Kinmel Bay

5

4

6

Rhyl

Towyn

0   1 km   1 mile

Difficulty rating

Time

▲ River, Sea, Castle, Birds, Great Views, Café, Food Shop, Good for Kids, Moor, Public Transport, Woodland, Ancient Monument

Three Cliffs Bay from Penmaen

This is a circular walk from Penmaen through the woods and moorland to Three Cliffs Bay on the south coast of the Gower peninsula, a designated area of outstanding natural beauty.

❶ Follow the track up the ridge. When you pass a stone marked 'Gower Way 12', bear right, following the track that skirts the woodland to your right. Just before the path divides, cross the stile on your right and follow the path into the woods as it opens out into a wider track. After a right-hand bend, go straight ahead at a crossroads (passing Gower Way stone 14).

❷ At the crossroads at the bottom of a valley, turn right, following the track down. (Opposite on the left is Gower Way stone 15.) The remnants of a prehistoric burial chamber will soon appear on your right.

❸ Go through the gateway following a yellow arrow. Ignore the road on the left but turn left at the T-junction. On reaching the Gower Heritage Centre, continue straight ahead and cross the footbridge on the left. Continue along the road until you reach the main road.

❹ Pass Shepherd's shop on your left and a house on your right. Turn right onto a path by a field gate. After 20 m, cross the footbridge and turn right, following a blue arrow. The path bears left over a hill. Ignore the left-hand path and continue ahead. The path opens out with a view of Pennard Castle. Continue down the left-hand side of the valley.

❺ As you near the beach, continue ahead until you reach a ridge of pebbles, then turn right along the ridge and cross the stepping-stones. Do not take the path ahead marked by an arrow but turn left. Continue around the edge of the marsh with the hedge on your right. Go to the left of the sand dunes and emerge onto the beach.

❻ Take the path to the top of the dunes. Follow the path that climbs up on the right-hand side of the holiday cottages. When you reach a stony track turn left, then turn right onto the road. Turn left at the T-junction. Cross the main road in front of the church and return to the start of the walk by following the narrow road on the right.

access information

Follow the A4118 along the Gower. Shortly after the Gower Inn at the Penmaen sign on the left-hand side, with the church in front of you, turn right on the narrow road. Follow this for about 200 yards, passing the care home on your left. When the road bears left, bear right onto the rough track and park on the grass.

Penmaen is accessible by bus service 18 from Swansea.

The view from the cliffs at Three Cliffs Bay in Swansea makes the climb up the sand dunes worthwhile.

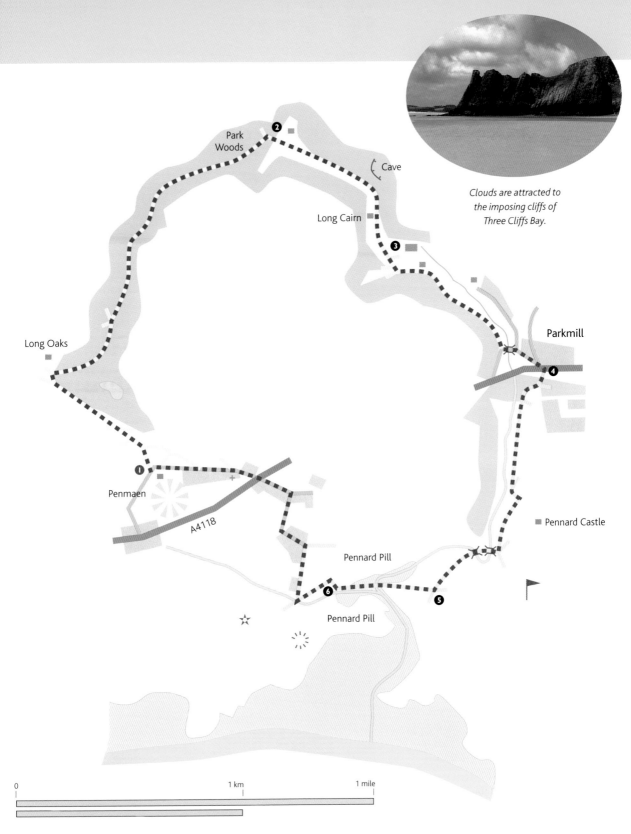

Park
Woods

Cave

Long Cairn

Clouds are attracted to
the imposing cliffs of
Three Cliffs Bay.

Parkmill

Long Oaks

Penmaen

Pennard Castle

A4118

Pennard Pill

Pennard Pill

0   1 km   1 mile

▲ Map: Explorer OL 35

▲ Distance: 7 km/4¼ miles

▲ Walk ID: 1411 Pat Roberts

Difficulty rating

Time

▲ Sea, Toilets, Wildlife, Birds, Flowers, Great Views, Butterflies, Woodland

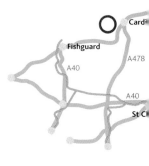

Witches' Cauldron from Moylgrove

This walk is a lovely mixture of coast and countryside, taking in two woodland areas.

❶ From the car park walk right along the road towards St Dogmaels. Follow the road as it climbs. Where the road swings sharply right, look for a gate on the left. Pass through the gate and walk down through Cwm Trewyddel, following the stream. The path goes over a small bridge and up to join the minor road from Moylgrove.

❷ Follow the road round the bend and up the hill for about 120 m. Follow the 'Coast Path' sign on the right, and continue with the sea on your right.

❸ Pwll y Wrach (The Witches' Cauldron) is a classic example of marine erosion. The path drops right down and climbs sharply back up, passing over a natural arch on the way. The sea comes in under the arch, creating the 'boiling cauldron'. Follow the path down the steps and back up the other side.

❹ After the climb you come to a double stile. Leave the coast by the left-hand stile. The route continues over fields initially. After passing a ruined building, enter the woodland of Cwm Ffynnon-alwm to emerge over a stile and turn left onto a green track. This soon becomes a stony farm track climbing gradually.

❺ Continue through a gate opposite Treriffith Farm where the sign points right, past the farm buildings then left up the drive. Emerge through a gate and continue to reach the Moylgrove road.

At the evocatively named Witches' Cauldron, the sea can be quite calm or spectacularly rough.

access information

Parking is in the car park at Moylgrove, a small village signed from the B4582 which is itself off the A487 Cardigan to Fishguard road.

▲ Map: Explorer OL 36
▲ Distance: 1.5 km/1 mile
▲ Walk ID: 1089 Peter Salenieks

Difficulty rating   Time

▲ Sea, Toilets, National Trust,
Wildlife, Birds, Flowers, Great Views,
Gift Shop, Mostly Flat, Public
Transport, Ancient Monument

Martin's Haven and Marine Nature Reserve

St David's
A487
A40
A40
Haverfordwest
Milford Haven
Pembroke Dock
A477   Tenby

This is a scenic circuit of the headland at Martin's Haven, offering views of Skomer Island and Skokholm Island and opportunities for watching seals within the Marine Nature Reserve.

❶ Exit the National Trust car park at the far corner. Walk down a few steps, then turn left and follow the road downhill towards Martin's Haven. Just before the road bends right, go through the kissing gate and turn left. Follow a grassy path, which runs parallel to the stone wall, until you see a stile near the cliff edge, overlooking Deadman's Bay.

❷ The path leads clockwise around the tip of the Marloes Peninsula. After the path bears around to the right, a natural arch can be seen, connecting two coves on the edge of the peninsula. About 200 m after the arch, the path joins a footpath, which leads to Wooltack Point, the northern tip of the peninsula.

❸ Retrace your route from Wooltack Point and bear left, following the footpath along the northern edge of the peninsula, before bearing right and climbing a small hill to reach the old coastguard lookout.

❹ Continue along the footpath until you reach steps leading down to the kissing gate. Go through the kissing gate and follow the road back uphill, passing Lockley Lodge Information Point, to reach the National Trust car park.

access information

The National Trust car park at Martin's Haven is accessible by road from Haverfordwest via the B4327 and a minor road through Marloes. Martin's Haven can also be reached by the Puffin Shuttle Bus Service 400, which operates between St David's and Milford Haven.

This footpath offers both rugged cliff views and a chance to spot grey seals.

Wooltack Point

Haven Point

Martin's Haven

Jack Sound

The Anvil

Deadman's Bay

0   1 km   1 mile

Woodland & Hillside

The Welsh mountains and forests offer a spectacular range of landscape and wildlife. Highlights include the Precipice Walk and the Brecon Beacons Horseshoe.

▲ Map: Explorer OL 17

▲ Distance: 14 km/8¾ miles

▲ Walk ID: 338 Haydn Williams

Difficulty rating

Time

▲ Pub, Castle, Great Views

Tal-y-Fan

This walk takes you over the northern part of the Carneddau range. Allow yourself time at the summit to enjoy this glorious landscape and also views of Anglesey, Liverpool and the Conwy Valley.

❶ From the car park follow the black track for half a kilometre. The way the tracks diverge is slightly confusing, but you should turn sharp right and follow the obvious track uphill. Keep the lake to your right and continue for half a kilometre, to meet a farmer's track.

❷ Turn right onto this track and stay on it until you reach a wall on the left, following it for about 2.5 km. Cross the ford, then continue uphill, keeping the wall on the right for 200 m. Pick up the track immediately ahead. Continue for about one kilometre, from where you will see a wall 90 degrees to your right.

❸ Turning right at this wall, and by keeping it on your left, you will start a steep climb for 200 m. On reaching the summit cross the ladder stile to the trig point.

❹ At the summit enjoy the extensive views of the Menai Straits, Anglesey, Puffin Island, Conwy Bay, Great Orme, Llandudno Bay, Conwy Castle and the Conwy Valley. Recross the ladder stile and go directly downhill with the wall at your back. When you reach a small cairn, turn right onto a footpath that takes you back to the wall. Follow this until you reach a distinct corner of the wall.

❺ From this point pick your own path down to the quarry, heading diagonally right for half a kilometre. At the quarry take the left-hand route down. After approximately 200 m a stream drops off to the right. Continue straight on and turn right at the next obvious path.

❻ Walk past the standing stone and this path will bring you back to your original track. Turn left and follow the track back to the car park.

The windswept ridges of the Welsh mountains offer panoramic views to take the breath away.

Pengychnant

Craigytedwen

access information

Conwy is on the A55 near Llandudno. By car from Conwy town square, turn left before the arch, proceed uphill to another arch and follow the road to the right, going uphill for 2 km. Go over the cattle grid and, ignoring the small car park by the road junction, carry on uphill. After a bend on the road you will see a well-built wall with a parking sign. Turn left here into the car park. To come by public transport use the Sherpa Park & Ride.

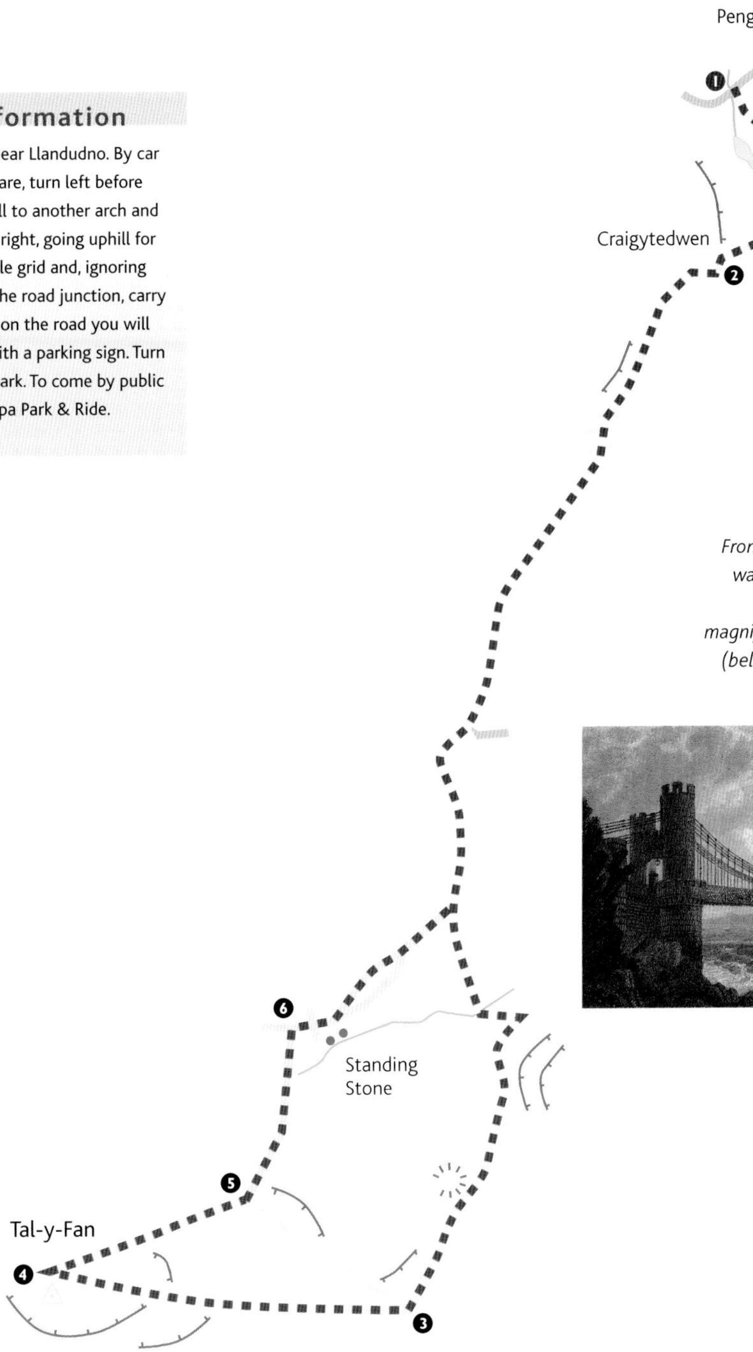

From the highest point of this walk you will have excellent views of Conwy, with its magnificent castle and a bridge (below) built to complement the style of the fortress.

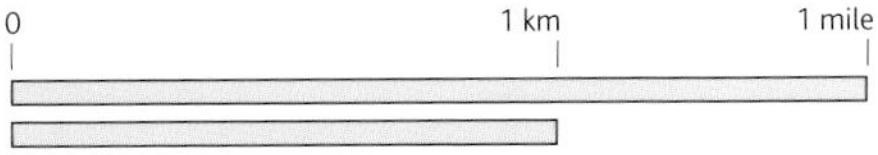

Standing Stone

Tal-y-Fan

0   1 km   1 mile

▲ Map: Explorer OL 17
▲ Distance: 8 km/5 miles
▲ Walk ID: 738 Jim Grindle

Difficulty rating

Time

▲ National Trust/NTS,
Great Views, Toilets

Bodnant Gardens and Moel Gyffylog

This walk begins at the attractive National Trust gardens at Bodnant. It covers the unclassified lanes to the east, rising to 250 m and offering outstanding views over the Conwy valley to the Carneddau range.

1 Turn left out of the car park at Bodnant. In 300 m you will come to a lane, Ffordd Bodnant. Turn left here and left again at the T-junction just ahead. The lane goes uphill for about 1.4 km to a junction just past Bodnant Ucha farm.

2 Turn right. In 350 m you reach a junction with another lane. Turn left here. Pass a junction with a lane from the left and continue to a small farm, Erw Goch. Barely 100 m further on there is another T-junction.

3 Turn right with the telephone lines on your right. At the top of the rise is another farm and 100 m beyond it you reach another T-junction. Turn left and go only 50 m, to a lane coming in from the right.

4 Turn right here for the next junction, 800 m away. Turn right at the signpost in the direction of Eglwysbach. It is 2.5 km downhill to the village, and you cross the stream by the entrance to Gyffylog farm on the way.

5 Turn right in Eglwysbach, to pass a bus stop on the left and a chapel on the right. Eight hundred metres from the junction you reach a red telephone box and a bus shelter by a crossroads in the hamlet of Graig. Bodnant is signposted on the right. Keep straight on, passing the bus shelter on your left.

6 Follow the road to Bodnant, to visit the gardens or return to the car park.

further information

The café, car park and the garden centre are free to enter but there is an entrance fee to the gardens themselves (NT members go in free). In addition to the beautiful gardens, there are many semi-wild areas and ponds. The grounds are open every day from mid-March to early November.

access information

Bodnant is on the A470 south of Llandudno and is well signposted from the A55. A bus from Conwy stops outside the gardens.

This walk starts at the lovely gardens at Bodnant.

▲ Map: Explorer OL 23
▲ Distance: 6 km/3¾ miles
▲ Walk ID: 225 Ian Morison

Difficulty rating

Time

▲ Hills or Fells, Lake/Loch, Toilets, Wildlife, Birds, Great Views

The Precipice Walk, north of Dolgellau

A classic Snowdonia walk with wonderful vistas over the Arans, Coed y Brenin Forest, the Mawddach estuary and Cader Idris. The view is one of the most beautiful panoramas in Wales, and there are perfect spots for picnics.

❶ Turn left out of the car park and follow the minor road for a short way. Turn left along the signposted track. Follow it round to the right where the track splits into two, keeping the open field to your left. Bear left as you pass the stone cottage.

❷ Cross a low ladder stile into woodland and turn right along the path. Cross the stile at the end of the wood into the open country. Follow the path round to the right. Llyn Cynwch is seen down the valley on the left.

❸ Turn right at the corner of the field following the signpost direction. Cross the ladder stile. The village of Llanfachreth is seen in the valley to your right. As you follow the stony path round to the left, Coed y Brenin Forest stretches out in front of you.

❹ The narrow path takes you along the flanks of Foel Cynwch. To the right lies the River Mawddach. The view opens out with the Mawddach estuary becoming visible to the right with distant views of Cader Idris.

❺ Climb over a ladder stile and follow the path round the hillside to the left. Cross a further ladder stile. Follow the path down towards Llyn Cynwch.

❻ Bear left, and drop onto the path by the lake. Follow the path beside the lake. Rejoin the outward route and retrace your steps to the car park.

access information

By car only. A National Park car park is on the left-hand side of the minor road between Dolgellau, on the A470, and the village of Llanfachreth – from Dolgellau, follow signs to the Precipice Walk.

further information

The route runs high above the River Mawddach. The ground drops steeply into the valley so young children will need to be well supervised, but there are no sheer drops. The path is good, but occasionally rocky.

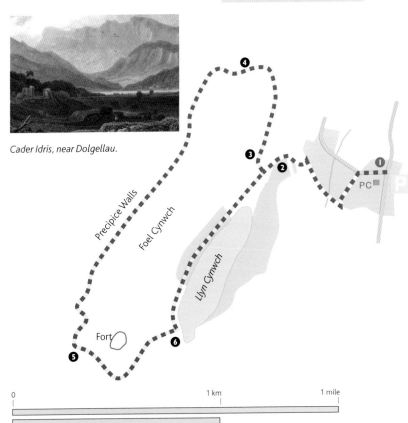

Cader Idris, near Dolgellau.

Difficulty rating

Time

River, Pub, Toilets, Church, Wildlife, Birds, Great Views, Café, Gift Shop, Tea Shop, Woodland

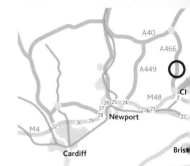

Devil's Pulpit from Tintern Abbey

This is a short walk from the atmospheric, ivy-clad ruins of Tintern Abbey along woodland paths that lead to the Devil's Pulpit, overlooking the Wye Valley. The route follows part of the Offa's Dyke Path.

❶ From the car park opposite Tintern Abbey, walk along a minor road that leads towards the River Wye. Pass the Anchor pub to reach a footpath on the left. Follow the footpath along the bank of the river. After the footpath turns towards Tintern, pass a whitewashed house on the left and continue along a minor road to reach a T-junction with the A466.

❷ Turn right and continue along the pavement, passing a hotel on your left and an art gallery on your right. Continue until you reach a minor road junction on your right, just past the Abbey Mill.

❸ Walk along the minor road towards the River Wye and cross the footbridge. Continue along the footpath, passing another footpath on the right. Follow the path on the left as it leads uphill, with several metal posts at the start. Shortly after it levels off, there is a junction. Take the right-hand path and follow it until you reach another junction marked by a wooden post with a footpath sign.

❹ Take the right-hand path. At the next junction, turn left and follow the footpath uphill. As the gradient levels off, the path bears to the right. Climb the short flight of wooden steps on the left to reach a junction marked by a wooden post with a footpath sign.

❺ Turn right and walk along the track. At the next junction bear left and follow the footpath uphill to reach Offa's Dyke Path. Turn right at the footpath sign and walk along Offa's Dyke Path until you reach a junction and a sign at a right-hand bend.

❻ Continue along Offa's Dyke Path from the footpath sign to reach the Devil's Pulpit. Retrace your route to the start.

Tintern Abbey, founded in 1131, was the first Cistercian monastery in Wales. Over the past 100 years it has undergone a continuous programme of maintenance and restoration.

access information

Tintern lies between Monmouth and Chepstow in the Wye Valley. The abbey is just off the A466, at the southern end of the village. There is a car park just off the main road. If this is full, the car park for Tintern Abbey is at the rear of the abbey, beside the River Wye.

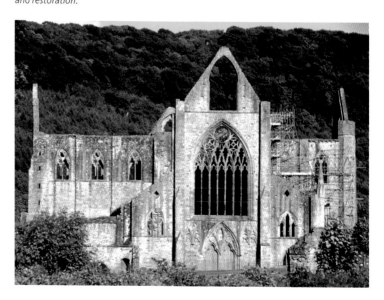

This walk can be combined with a visit to Tintern Abbey. Contact the information centre on 01291 689251 for information about when the abbey is open.

The Devil's Pulpit is a small limestone rock that juts out from the cliffs. It looks down over Tintern Abbey from the hills beside Offa's Dyke on the eastern side of the River Wye. Local legend has it that the Devil stood upon the Devil's Pulpit to preach to the monks below, tempting them to desert their order.

The view of Tintern Abbey from the Devil's Pulpit takes in a vast expanse of the River Wye.

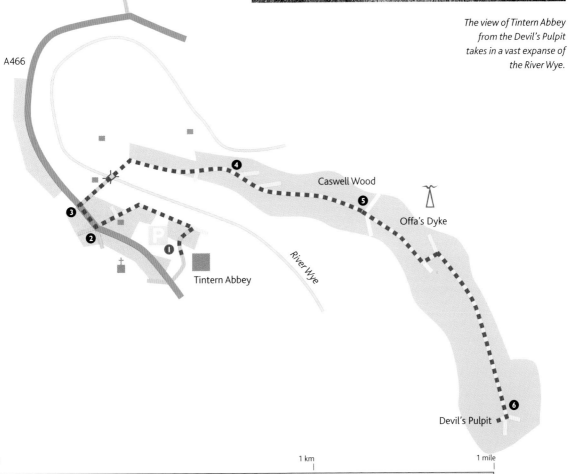

A466

Caswell Wood

Offa's Dyke

River Wye

Tintern Abbey

Devil's Pulpit

0   1 km   1 mile

▲ Map: Explorer OL 35
▲ Distance: 11 km/6¾ miles
▲ Walk ID: 1323 Pat Roberts

Difficulty rating

Time

▲ Mountains, Wildlife, Birds, Flowers,
Great Views, Butterflies, Moor, Tea
Shop, Woodland

Carningli from Sychbant

This walk climbs to Bedd Morris, then on to Carningli, for incredible views of the Wicklow Hills in Ireland, the Welsh coast and the Preseli Hills, to return down through the Gwaun Valley.

❶ From the car park walk up the drive to Ffald-y-Brenin (Sychbant on the map). Where the drive swings left, go over the marked stile to the left of the gate. Continue up a field to pass through another gate. Turn left to reach a gate with blue arrows. Go through the gate and turn right up a green lane. Go over two stiles in quick succession to enter the forest. An information board tells us that this is the 'Penlan Project'. Follow the arrow to the right, to Carningli. After about 1 km bear left towards Bedd Morris and emerge from the forest on a stony track.

❷ At Bedd Morris, with the stone behind you, walk ahead on a path that follows a raised bank in an easterly direction, leaving the bank to curve slightly left over the top of Mynydd Caregog. After passing above the forest, a fence comes in from the right. Follow the grassy path, keeping the fence on your right. As you come level with Carn Edward, a large rocky outcrop on the right, take the left fork, then turn immediately left again.

❸ Keep heading towards Carningli, following any of the small paths. Once you are within 150 m of the outcrop, head for the northern end, and you will see a well-used route up onto the top.

❹ At the top of Carningli there are fantastic views. Retrace your steps off the outcrop, and turn right. Take the most suitable path round the rocks. Descend on the narrow but good path heading east. Follow the path down to the Dolrannog road.

❺ On reaching the road turn right. Go through the farmyard and walk through a metal gate to pass Dolrannog Uchaf.

❻ At the end of the road go through the gate to the left of the bungalow. Follow the bridle path down through the woods to reach Llanerch and the valley road. Turn right to return to the start.

further information

There are many legends attached to Bedd Morris, but it is most likely a Bronze Age standing stone and is now one of the markers standing on Newport Parish Boundary.

An ancient copper-beech tree presides over the Preseli Hills like a monument to the enduring power of nature.

With its weather-beaten rocks, standing stones and ancient legends, Carningli is not a place for the faint-hearted.

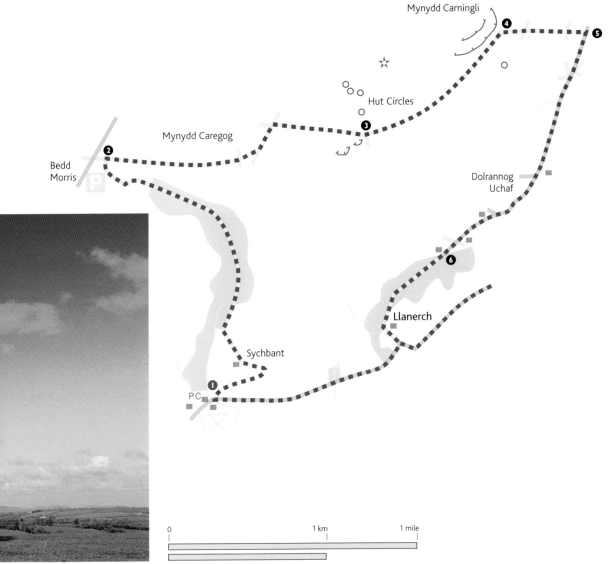

Mynydd Carningli

Hut Circles

Mynydd Caregog

Bedd Morris

Dolrannog Uchaf

Sychbant

Llanerch

P C

0   1 km   1 mile

▲ Map: Explorer OL 12

▲ Distance: 11 km/6¾ miles

▲ Walk ID: 1290 John Thorn

Difficulty rating

Time

▲ Mountains, Reservoir, National Trust, Wildlife, Birds, Flowers, Great Views

Brecon Beacons Horseshoe

This walk to the top of the Brecon Beacons has stupendous views from almost every point.

❶ Do not go through the gate but turn up to the right to reach a track. Cross the stile and walk between the two fences. When the fence on your right turns right follow it up. As you approach the trees bear left to join the rough track. Turn left onto the Roman road. Go down a steep dip and up the other side, bearing right. Follow the track to the top of the pass.

❷ At the top, cross the stile on your left and bear left on the well-defined path that climbs around the shoulder of Cribyn. At the saddle between Cribyn and Pen y Fan, continue ahead, climbing steeply. Look over your right shoulder for views of Cribyn, Llangorse Lake, the Black Mountains and, later, the Sugar Loaf.

❸ The summit of Pen y Fan has commanding views in all directions. Descend towards the flat top of Corn Du, but at the saddle bear left. At the next saddle bear left again, climbing slightly to follow the escarpment for about 3 km. You pass to the left of a large cairn, following the edge. Pass another large cairn and ignore the steep path down to your left in a fold in the mountain.

❹ Turn right to start a steep descent, aiming for the end of the dam. Go though the gate, walk along the dam then veer off to the right to cross a bridge. Go through the gate to reach the starting point.

access information

Start at the parking area by the dam of the lower Neuadd reservoir. Access is from the minor road between Vaynor/Merthyr and Talybont off the A465.

The Brecon Beacons.

further information

Pen y Fan is the highest point in South Wales. Do not attempt this walk in poor visibility. Most of the paths on the first part are well defined but become less so after leaving Corn Du, and parts of the route can be very muddy or boggy.

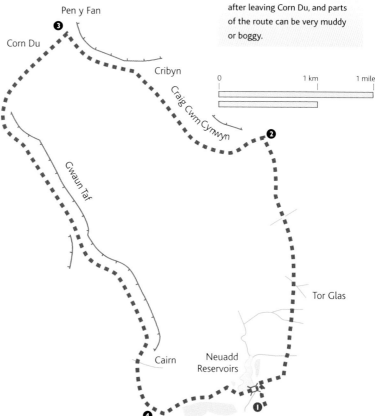

▲ Map: Explorer 200
▲ Distance: 9 km/5½ miles
▲ Walk ID: 951 Pete Brett

Difficulty rating
!!!

Time
●●●

▲ Hills or Fells, Reservoir, Toilets, Play Area, Church, Wildlife, Birds, Flowers, Great Views, Good for Wheelchairs, Nature Trail, Tea Shop, Woodland

Garreg-ddu Reservoir from Elan Valley

This relatively short walk offers the walker peace and tranquillity amid superb scenery, with the opportunity to enjoy breathtaking views.

1 Leave the car park taking the ascending path to a cinder track and turn left towards Caban Coch Dam. Remain on the track beside the reservoir until you reach the arched road bridge.

2 Cross the road by Foel Tower and rejoin the track. (If time permits you can turn left over the road bridge and visit Nantgwyllt Church on the far bank.) Leave the track through the gate and continue on the grass verge beside the road for 200 m to the bridle path on the right. Climb the bridle path steeply at first then over the stream, ignoring any small side tracks.

3 Where the path branches left, continue straight ahead towards high ground for all-round views. From the viewpoint return to this point and descend the path, following small posts and signs to reach a metal gate.

4 At the gate turn right and continue to descend, following little yellow markers until you reach a wire fence. Turn left and follow the fence to the gates of the water treatment buildings. Go through the gates and down steps to the road.

5 Cross the road. Behind the houses, cross the footbridge over the river. Turn right and follow the river through the Elan estate to pass the toilets on the left. Go through a white gate beside the bridges into Cnwch woods and continue on the path through the trees.

6 Go behind the first turbine house and cross the bridge in front of the dam. Head behind the second turbine house to return to the visitor centre car park.

The bridge over the majestic Caban Coch Dam forms an integral part of this walk.

access information

From Rhayader take the B4518 road heading south-west (follow signs to Elan Valley Reservoirs) and park at the Elan Valley Visitor Centre.

further information

Wheelchair users can follow the route alongside the reservoirs, returning to the visitor centre the same way.

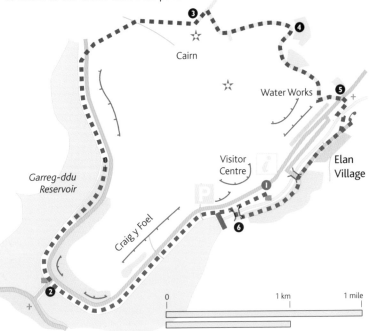

South-west England

Coastal & Waterside

This is a region of delightful bays and secret coves, with monuments that invoke all manner of myths and legends. Highlights include Tintagel, Lulworth Cove and Old Harry.

▲ Map: Explorer OL 20

▲ Distance: 4 km/2½ miles

▲ Walk ID: 995 Dennis Blackford

Difficulty rating

Time

▲ Hills or Fells, Sea, Wildlife, Birds, Flowers, Great Views, Butterflies, Industrial Archaeology

Scabbacombe Coast – Two Bays Walk

This is another pleasant walk taking in part of the South West Coast Path and visiting the two bays of Man Sands and Scabbacombe Sands. It is a fairly short walk, so you will have plenty of time to relax on the beach if you wish.

1 Leave the car park and turn right into the road. Follow the road down about 1 km to Man Sands car park. Continue past Man Sands car park. The tarmac road now continues as a stony track. As you near the beach, the path branches to the right. Continue straight on to Man Sands Beach. Return to the branch and walk up a side-shoot for about 100 m to reach a stile on your right. The stone structure that you pass on the way to the beach is an old limekiln where lime was baked to make fertilizer.

2 Go into the field via the stile. The path is clearly signposted and passes behind the old coastguard cottages. Walk up the path and through the gap in the wall.

3 Take the path up the hill to the top of the field. Walk south along the South West Coast Path, bearing around to your right and along to the gate.

4 Pass through the gate or over the stile and follow the coast path for about another kilometre to reach another gate and stile.

5 After passing through the gate, continue along the coast path for about 400 m until you come to a stile over the fence, leading to Scabbacombe Beach. After spending some time on the beach, return up the path to the stile. Walk back along the coast about 200 m and slightly up to the left, until you come to an isolated stile with no fence. Turn left here and follow the sheep path to the main gate leading into the farm track.

6 Pass through the gate or over the stile onto the farm track. At the top of the farm track, pass the large gate and go through the kissing gate back to the car park.

access information

By car, take the Brixham to Kingswear road. About 1.5 km from the small roundabout, halfway down a hill past the holiday camp, turn left, signposted 'Kingston, Boohay, Woodhuish and Brownstone'. After about 1.5 km, this lane branches into two lanes with dead-end signs. Take the left-hand one. Just under 1 km away, an opening in the hedgerow on the right leads into the car park.

By bus, take the Brixham to Kingswear bus to the end of the above lane. It is about 2 km from the bus stop to the car park.

further information

The left-hand end of Scabbacombe is a 'clothes optional' beach.

The rugged coastline between Brixham and Scabbacombe.

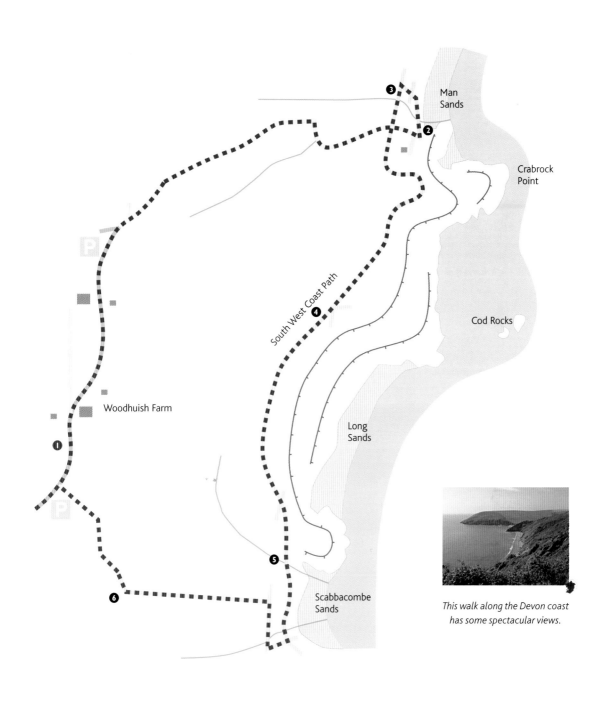

Man
Sands

Crabrock
Point

❸

❷

Cod Rocks

South West Coast Path

❹

Woodhuish Farm

❶

Long
Sands

❺

❻

Scabbacombe
Sands

*This walk along the Devon coast
has some spectacular views.*

0   1 km   1 mile

Difficulty rating

Time

▲ Sea, Pub, Toilets, Museum, Church, Stately Home, Wildlife, Flowers, Great Views, Food Shop, Good for Kids, Tea Shop

South West Coast Path from Padstow

further information

The Elizabethan manor house of Prideaux Place has a deer park and is open to visitors in summer.

The church of St Petroc, dating mainly from the 15th century, and the Shipwreck Museum can both be found in Padstow.

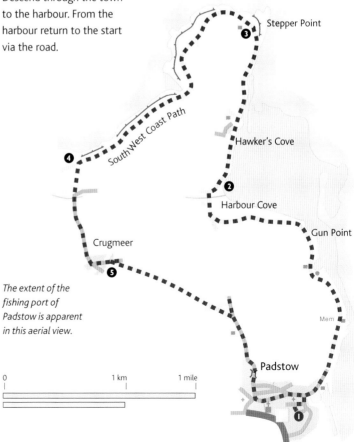

This is a circular walk from the Cornish fishing port of Padstow, with long stretches of sandy beach ideal for swimming, and dramatic cliff-top views.

❶ Leave the car park on the path to the left of the toilet block and descend to the north side of the harbour. Join the South West Coast Path, which starts near the tourist information centre. The path ascends to the War Memorial with extensive views back towards Padstow and the Camel Estuary. Follow the path around Gun Point to the beautiful sandy Harbour Cove.

❷ Cross the sands to rejoin the path. At Hawker's Cove the path joins a short stretch of track behind the beach and skirts the old lifeboat house and terraced pilots' houses.

❸ Ascend from the pilots' houses over the stile and take the right path to Stone Daymark. Continue on the coast path above dramatic cliffs with outstanding views.

❹ At the stile, turn left inland to reach a road. Follow the road to the village of Crugmeer and curve round to the left at the junction. Pass the cottages on the left and take the next left turn.

❺ Take the footpath on the right, just past Little Crugmeer Farm. Cross the stile into the field. Cross diagonally over seven fields with slate stiles to a stile leading onto the road. Turn right along the road and under the arch to Prideaux Place. Continue down the road and turn left at the hotel into Fentonluna Lane. Descend through the town to the harbour. From the harbour return to the start via the road.

access information

Follow the A39 south from Wadebridge then take the A389 to Padstow. Do not descend into the town but continue for 200 m and turn into the top car park.

The extent of the fishing port of Padstow is apparent in this aerial view.

0   1 km   1 mile

▲ Map: Explorer 111
▲ Distance: 3 km/1¾ miles
▲ Walk ID: 1095 Dennis Blackford

Difficulty rating

Time

▲ Hills or Fells, Sea, Toilets, Castle,
National Trust, Wildlife, Birds,
Flowers, Great Views, Butterflies,
Restaurant, Tea Shop, Monument

Tintagel Castle and Coast

This walk goes through Tintagel and along the cliff path to visit the legendary castle of King Arthur and Merlin's Cave, with wonderful views and a wealth of wildlife.

❶ From the car park, turn right onto the main road and walk into Tintagel village. Walk through the village until reaching the 'No Through Road' at the side of the Cornishman's Inn. Follow this road down to the car park at the end.

❷ Follow the church wall around to the right and onto the coast path, looking out for the ruins of the castle below. Follow the path down.

❸ On reaching the paved path to the castle, take the path to your right which zigzags down to the Visitor Centre. At low tide you can go down to the beach and visit Merlin's Cave.

❹ Cross over the bridge and climb the steps to continue on the coast path up the other side of the valley. About 200 m further on, after crossing a little wooden bridge, follow the left-hand path up to Barras Nose, with its spectacular view over the cove and the castle. Continue on the coast path. About 1 km further on, pass through a gate which will lead you to Willapark. Pass through the gap in the wall and take the left-hand fork to the point. Return to the junction and

With natural and man-made rock formations, it is no wonder Tintagel is a place of legends.

continue on the path to the right of the gap, heading down into the valley.

❺ Take the steps up the other side of the valley and cross the stile down to the track. Turn right to return to the starting point.

access information

Tintagel is on the B3263 off the A39. From Tintagel, take the Boscastle road for about 1 km to Bossiney car park on your left.

There are also bus services to take you to Tintagel.

further information

At waymark 5, instead of turning right, you could turn left to detour down into the secluded cove of Bossiney Haven, which is popular for swimming at low tide.

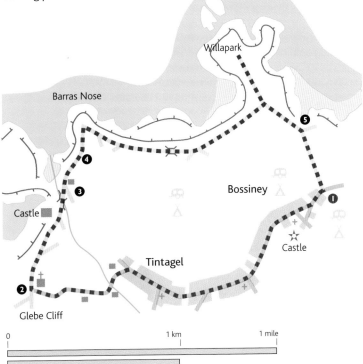

▲ Map: Explorer 105
▲ Distance: 7 km/4¼ miles
▲ Walk ID: 1513 Jim Grindle

Difficulty rating

Time

▲ River, Toilets, Stately Home, National Trust, Wildlife, Birds, Good for Kids, Nature Trail, Restaurant, Tea Shop, Woodland, Ancient Monument

Lamouth Creek from Trelissick Garden

You begin by entering the park and dropping down to follow the river through woods to King Harry Ferry. The walk offers open views of the estuary before a gentle climb through the park back to the start.

1 Take the path next to the car park, signposted 'Woodland Walks'. Go through a gate next to a cattle grid and follow the path to a junction. Turn right onto the driveway and continue to the edge of a wood.

2 Go through the gate to the left of the cattle grid, then turn to the right on a path going uphill. Pass the lodge and go through the green gate. Cross the road and go through the gate on the other side. Follow a gravel track that zigzags downhill. When it straightens out there is a stream on the left.

3 Turn left and cross the stream. On the other side take the right fork, following Lamouth Creek, which is below you on your right. Continue as the woods thin out, until you reach the entrance to the next wood, marked by two low stone banks. Take the right fork, heading over the ditch and then straight through the rampart of the Iron Age fort before joining another track. Turn right. Just before the quay, go down a few steps and emerge into the open.

4 Visit Roundwood Quay, then retrace your steps back to point 3. Continue with the river now on your left for 1.5 km. You will reach a steep flight of steps leading down to the road you crossed earlier. The ferry is just to your left, and opposite is a white house with a flight of steps going up on its right.

5 At Bosanko's Cottage, take the track that continues on the far side. Only one track branches off to the right away from the river and your way is signposted. About 1.5 km from the ferry you leave the woods by a kissing gate. Go up the hill, keeping the iron fence on your right.

6 At the top cross the drive that enters Trelissick House. You will soon reach the exit from the car park. Go through the gate and back to the start.

access information

Trelissick is 6 km south of Truro on the B3289, east of the A39. Buses T7 and 89B run from Truro, where there is a railway station.

This footpath will lead you past cosy woodland cottages to the much grander residence of Trelissick House.

further information

The first house was built here in about 1750 and went through many hands, with much development of the gardens which were acquired by The National Trust in 1955.

Roundwood Quay was built in the 18th century to ship tin and copper, and in past days there were buildings for smelting and refining and many wharves. There was a malt house, limekilns and ship-building yards, a busy place compared to the tranquillity that you will find there now.

Since 1888 the King Harry Steam Ferry Company has operated a ferry that pulls itself across the Fal by chains, although the motive power is now diesel. It is thought that a ferry has existed here since the Norman Conquest.

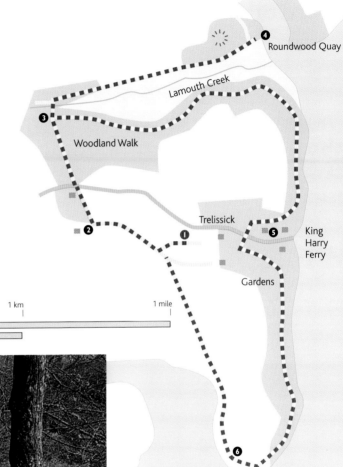

▲ Map: Explorer OL 15
▲ Distance: 15 km/9¼ miles
▲ Walk ID: 389 Al Rodger

Difficulty rating

Time

▲ Hills or Fells, Sea, Pub, Toilets, Wildlife, Great Views

Lulworth and White Nothe Coastal Tour

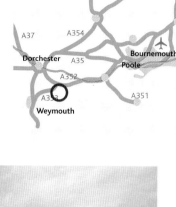

Starting on the ridge above Ringstead, the route first crosses downland to West Lulworth and the magnificent coast at Lulworth Cove and Durdle Door, to return along the cliff-top path.

❶ Exit the car park over the stile at the far end and continue down the track. Where the track bears sharp right, cross the stile and continue up the track. Keep straight ahead through two more stiles and a gate.

❷ At the second gate, keep straight ahead over the next two rises. As the path rises for a third time, turn right over the stile at the signpost to Newlands Farm Camp Site. Go through Newlands Farm and continue past West Lulworth Church and down to Lulworth Cove.

❸ The walk resumes from the pay-and-display car park up Hambury Tout on the stone path, dropping down to the cliff above Durdle Door, then over the small hill to Scratchy Bottom.

❹ From Scratchy Bottom cross the stile at the foot of Swyre Head and follow the path diagonally uphill. Cross the stile at the top, to reach a well-used path. Follow the path until reaching the obelisk.

❺ At the obelisk, take one of the paths round the hillside and over the summit to the coastguard cottages at White Nothe. Continue along the cliff top, with Weymouth Bay in sight ahead. Cross the stile and descend the field onto a track at the next stile.

❻ Follow the track uphill, bearing left at a post box. Continue ahead to the car park.

The stretch of coastline between Durdle Door and Lulworth Cove is possibly the most impressive in the whole of Dorset.

access information

This walk starts from the Ringstead Bay National Trust car park on the ridge above Ringstead. Take the Ringstead turning off the A353 between Poxwell and Osmington. Follow the road ahead to the car park, parking towards the far end.

No practical access by public transport.

▲ Map: Explorer 102
▲ Distance: 6½ km/4 miles
▲ Walk ID: 124 Colin Ward

Difficulty rating

Time

▲ Sea, Pub, Great Views

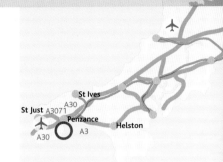

Lamorna Cove from Mousehole

This walk takes you from the picturesque fishing village of Mousehole to Lamorna, returning along the South West Coast Path.

❶ From the harbour, take the lane past the Lobster Pot restaurant to the Methodist chapel. Walk up the hill, out of the village, to the point where it bears to the right. Keep on the road for about 100 m, and follow the footpath sign to take a path on the left.

❷ Turn right into the field and walk round the edge, until you reach the stile on the far side. Continue walking across the field to reach the farm at Kemyel Drea. The path passes to the right of the first building, and then between the large sheds. Once through the farm, follow the hedge and pick up the path that leads into the hedges beyond.

❸ Walk to the stile and turn left. Continue straight up the lane past the farmhouses, and the gate marked with a Caravan Club sign. Cross the stile, and continue across the fields to the farmhouses of Kemyel Wartha. Follow the track through the hamlet, as it bears right to the footpath sign. Take the path on the left down to the quarry. Continue past the quarry to Lamorna Cove.

❹ Take the obvious path up to Carn-du and continue round the coast for 3 km. Eventually you will come to the road, where you should continue straight on, and down into Mousehole.

further information

The disued quarry on the way to Lamorna Cove supplied the stone for London Bridge. The cove was once used for shipping the stone, but the difficult task of navigating the harbour rendered it redundant in the last century.

The South West Coast Path goes through a small wooded nature reserve.

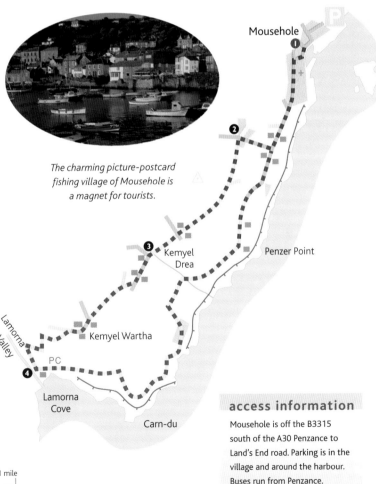

The charming picture-postcard fishing village of Mousehole is a magnet for tourists.

access information

Mousehole is off the B3315 south of the A30 Penzance to Land's End road. Parking is in the village and around the harbour. Buses run from Penzance.

0   1 km   1 mile

▲ Map: Explorer OL 15
▲ Distance: 10 km/6¼ miles
▲ Walk ID: 365 Al Rodger

Difficulty rating

Time

▲ Sea, Toilets, Church, National Trust, Wildlife, Birds, Flowers, Great Views

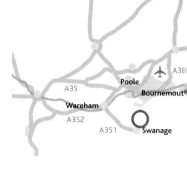

Old Harry and Ballard Down from Studland

A circular walk from Studland to Old Harry passing Studland's Norman church en route. Continuing up the coast and along the top of Ballard Down, the route returns to Studland via Agglestone Rock.

❶ Exit the car park away from the beach, immediately turning left at the road junction past the car park sign. Turn right at the road junction by the Manor House Hotel. Turn left through the gate and follow the path past St Nicholas's Church and continue straight ahead to the marker post. Turn left down the road and, where the road bends left, continue up the track straight ahead to the right of the public toilets. Keep straight ahead to Old Harry, where tracks join at a marker stone.

❷ The route continues up the cliff path. Keep outside the fenced area ahead and pause to sample the views behind you. Continue along the South West Coast Path. Keep left at the marker stone, taking in the superior views as you go.

❸ At the fence line coming in from the right, bear right away from the cliff and go through the gate and gap in the ancient dyke. Continue along the crest of Ballard Down.

❹ At the obelisk, continue straight ahead through the gate and down the track that bends to the right down to the road. Turn left down the road. Take the path on the right. Go over two stiles and through the woods, straight over the golf course to reach the stile onto the road.

access information

Studland is on the B3351 east of the A351. The walk starts from Middle Beach car park, situated at the end of Beach Road, the northern of the two side roads heading towards the beach.

A bus runs hourly from Bournemouth to Swanage over the ferry and stops at the end of Beach Road.

This chalk arch and stack form a spectacular view at the heart of Studland Bay.

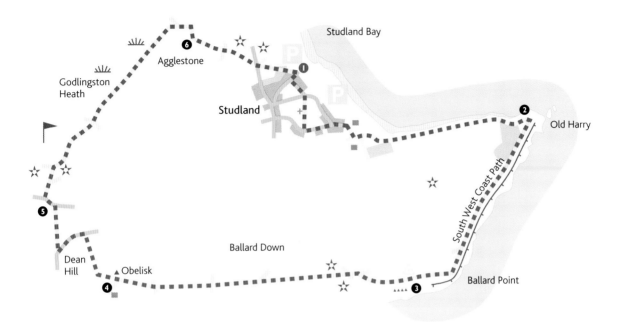

Studland Bay

Godlingston Heath

Agglestone

Studland

Old Harry

South West Coast Path

Ballard Down

Dean Hill

Obelisk

Ballard Point

0   1 km   1 mile

The Agglestone Rock (composed of sandstone in an area of limestone) is said to have been thrown at Corfe Castle by the Devil from the Isle of Wight.

⑤ Meander left and then right. Pass through two gates onto the good path. Keep straight ahead at the first two marker stones making for Agglestone Studland Heath. Turn left onto a bridle path just before the 'No Entry' signs, skirting the edge of the golf course. At the gate continue straight ahead on towards Agglestone. From Agglestone, the route continues down into the valley, ascending the far side before bearing right and descending again. At the main track, turn right downhill. The track turns sharply to the right and crosses a ford.

⑥ Continue up the track and through the gate, turning right at the main road. Cross the road and follow the path on the left through the gully to Beach Road. Turn left to return to the car park.

further information

St Nicholas's Church has been described as 'the most exciting building in Purbeck'. It is Norman, built on the remnants of a Saxon church destroyed by the Danes.

Old Harry is the large stack at the end of The Foreland. Sea birds abound at The Foreland, as do land species in the nature reserve on the cliff top. The spot with its views was special enough for the author H.G. Wells to have his ashes scattered here.

The obelisk at point 4 was brought to Swanage from London as ship's ballast. It was positioned on top of the Bronze Age barrow to commemorate the first piped water supply into Swanage.

Legend has it that Agglestone Rock was thrown here from the Isle of Wight by the Devil, who was aiming at Old Harry or Corfe Castle.

Woodland and hillside footpaths reveal historic West Country monuments and idyllic Cotswold villages. Highlights include Nancledra, Hardy's Chess Piece and Glastonbury Tor.

▲ Map: Explorer 102

▲ Distance: 7 km/4¼ miles

▲ Walk ID: 1038 Dennis Blackford

Difficulty rating

Time

▲ Hills or Fells, Lake/Loch, Wildlife, Birds, Flowers, Great Views, Butterflies, Industrial Archaeology, Moor, Ancient Monument

Nancledra

further information

From Roger's Tower there are fine views and you are surrounded by the ancient hill fort of Castle-an-Dinas.

Redruth

St Ives

St Just A307

A30

Penzance

Helston

A394

This moorland walk to the ancient hill fort of Castle-an-Dinas and Roger's Tower, a folly built in 1798, offers superb views over St Michael's Mount and Penzance bay.

1 Leave the car park and turn left down the main road to the junction. Turn right and continue up the country road.

2 Cross a small bridge and turn left at a branch in the road. Look for a house called The Moors and take the farm track to the right of the house. Continue to the top of the hill.

3 When you reach the junction, take the left-hand track until you come to a large house with a footpath to the right. Follow the path through a gate into a field. Cross the field to another gate in the top left-hand corner. Pass through the gate into another field and walk straight ahead to another gate leading into a large field.

4 Cross the field to pass through a pair of gates, turn right onto the track and continue for about 800 m. At the chimney, turn left onto a wide track. Continue past an old engine house. After about 300 m turn right through a break in the wall. Turn left and follow the track round until it ends in a field near a pile of rocks. Cross the field diagonally right to reach a track leading to a gate with a stile. Cross the stile and turn left. Continue up to reach a wide track.

5 Turn left and stay on the main track, which curves to the left at the new quarry. Go through the gate and walk along the quarry until you arrive at a path leading to Roger's Tower.

6 After visiting the tower, return to the track along the quarry rim and turn left. The track goes through a gateway in a wall, becoming a rough path. At the end of the quarry, head downhill. Go through the gate and bear right across the moor. Continue across a telegraph pole on the ground, through a wide gap in the hedge and onto a farm track. Head to the right towards the farmhouse.

7 Go through the gate by the farm and turn right, following the road to the main road. Turn left and walk back to the start.

access information

There is a bus service number 16 from St Ives and Penzance stopping in the village.

Nancledra is midway (about 6 km) on the B3311 road from St Ives to Penzance. On entering this small village watch for the tiny post office on the left. Turn up the track a little past the post office, which leads to the village car park.

St Michael's Mount, a former Benedictine priory and castle, is now the home of the St Aubyn family.

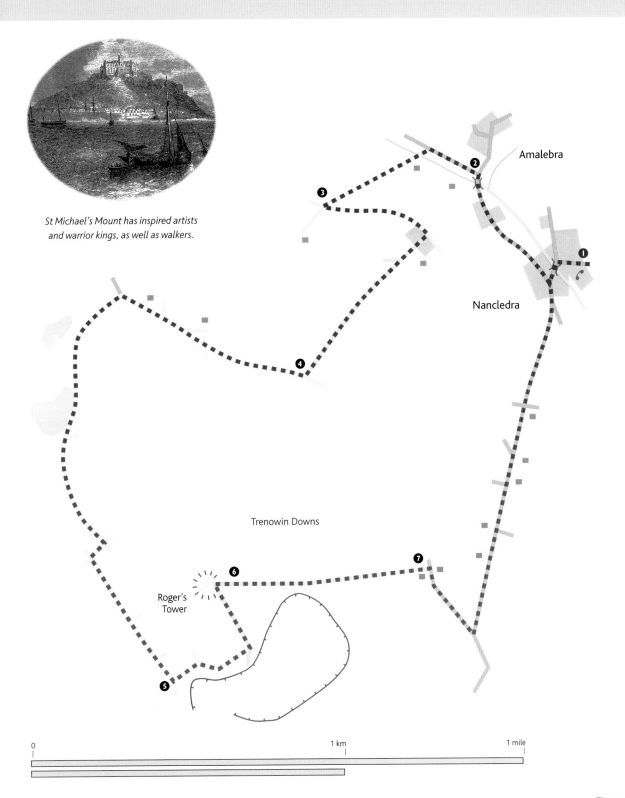

St Michael's Mount has inspired artists and warrior kings, as well as walkers.

Amalebra

Nancledra

Trenowin Downs

Roger's Tower

0   1 km   1 mile

▲ Map: Explorer 116

▲ Distance: 10 km/6¼ miles

▲ Walk ID: 997 Al Rodger

Difficulty rating

Time

▲ Pub, Church, Wildlife, Birds, Great Views, Butterflies, Woodland

Symondsbury from North Chideock

This is a circular walk through countryside west of Bridport, starting from the village of Chideock, home of the Chideock Martyrs. The route illustrates the charm of West Dorset at its best, and there are wonderful views to enjoy.

❶ Take the track with a cul-de-sac sign beside the cottage. Proceed uphill in a field with a fence on the left. Descend straight down the second field.

❷ Turn right up the hedged track. At the top of the hill continue down the Symondsbury track. Take the road to the left at the school.

❸ Beyond Symondsbury, turn right onto a track. Cross into a field on the left and make for the far-left corner. Cross the bridge and turn right, following the edge of the field to a gate. Cross the track into the field opposite. Cross the field half-left up to the corner of the hedge. Continue with the hedge on your right. At the hole through the hedge, take the path through the trees. Turn right at the junction. On the brow of the hill, turn left for rewarding views.

❹ Continue clockwise round the edge of the hilltop. Take the left path at the first junction. Continue down the steps towards the road and turn left. Turn right up the path between the housing and the hospital. Cross to the right-hand field. Keep ahead to cross back to the left-hand field at the gateway. Continue with the hedge on your right-hand side for two fields.

further information

John Cornelius, the Catholic chaplain of Lady Arundell, was arrested when visiting Chideock in 1594, along with two servants from Chideock and another visitor. The four were found guilty of treason. Refusing to embrace Protestantism, they were executed three months after their arrest.

A cross on the site of Chideock Castle commemorates these martyrs, and two others, Thomas Pilchard and Hugh Green.

The chiselled headlands around Lyme Regis create quite a distinctive coastline that is a fascinating place to explore.

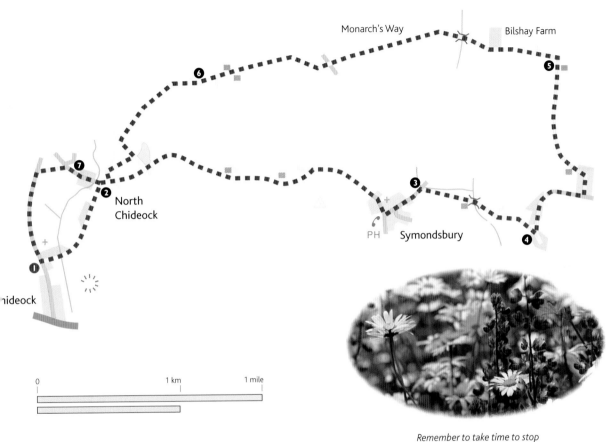

Monarch's Way

Bilshay Farm

❻

❺

❼

North Chideock

❷

❸

PH **Symondsbury**

❹

❶

hideock

| 0 | 1 km | 1 mile |

Remember to take time to stop on your walk and 'smell the flowers'.

❺ At the cottage turn left and follow the hedge. Cross the field to the right-hand of two gates into the next field. Head left towards the electricity pylon. Go over the stile into a garden, following the fence. Descend the field to a gate at the end of a line of posts. Cross the bridge and keep to the right side of the field. Go through the gap in the hedge into the next field. Follow the track up the left side to continue on the Monarch's Way.

❻ Go through both gates. Continue down the field and round the thicket on the sheep path. Follow the path and continue down the field towards the hedge, keeping the hedge on the right. Cross the bottom field to the left to reach a stile by a gate. Turn right to follow a track becoming a tarmac lane.

❼ Just before the junction, turn up the path on the left. Cross the field to a stile leading down to a path. Turn left at the road and continue back to the start.

access information

Turn north off the A35 in Chideock, west of Bridport, by the church on the road signed North Chideock. Just past the lane with the lodge on the corner, park on the side of the road with a slight verge.

A good bus service runs between Bridport and Lyme Regis and stops in Chideock, not far from the start.

▲ Map: Explorer OL 15

▲ Distance: 10 km/6¼ miles

▲ Walk ID: 572 Alan Kingsland

Difficulty rating

Time

▲ Hills or Fells, River, Pub, Church, National Trust, Wildlife, Birds, Flowers, Great Views

Hardy's Chess Piece Monument from Martinstown

This walk starts and finishes at St Martin's Church in the village of Martinstown, Dorset. The walk takes you through some fields and a copse to Great Hill. The walk then follows the ridge to the 'Chess Piece' that is Hardy's Monument.

❶ Cross the road from the church, then the footbridge to continue on a road. Once past the buildings the road bends first left then right. On the right bend join a footpath to the left. From the footpath sign the path leads across the field ahead. On the far side of this field go through a second to reach a young copse. Follow the path to the bottom of the valley. Then keep right as you travel up the valley to a farm track. Turn left, following the track to a field at the bottom of Great Hill.

❷ Take the chalky track up the first slope of Great Hill and into a field. Cross the middle of the field and go through the gate at the end. Continue across the next field to a hedge and signpost. Down to your left are views of Weymouth and Portland. Turn right and follow the path along the field edge and under the power lines. Take the path ahead at the rusty tanks. Go through a gate, up the hill between the gorse bushes to a second gate. Turn right and go through the gate, following the ridge path to Hardy's Chess Piece Monument. At the road turn left and follow it up to the car park and the monument.

❸ Retrace your steps back to the inland coastal path. Keep on the path to the junction.

❹ Turn left and follow the path to the farm buildings and road. At the road go through the gate and turn left. Follow this road to Pen Barn Farm.

❺ At the farm follow the path to the right, passing in front of the dark barn. Climb to the hilltop. Go through the gate and follow the field-edge path down the slope to the next gate and track.

❻ Turn left onto the track, leaving to the right after a very short distance. Follow the footpath back down the valley to the copse you passed earlier. Retrace your steps to St Martin's Church.

access information

From the A35 roundabout west of Dorchester, follow signposts to Martinstown. Turn right into the village and head for St Martin's Church (500 m on the right).

Located on the highest point of the Blackdown area, the 21-m Hardy's Monument is a landmark for any walker. Its site provides excellent views of the Dorset coast.

This footpath will lead you through some classic Dorset countryside, taking in picturesque villages and farms.

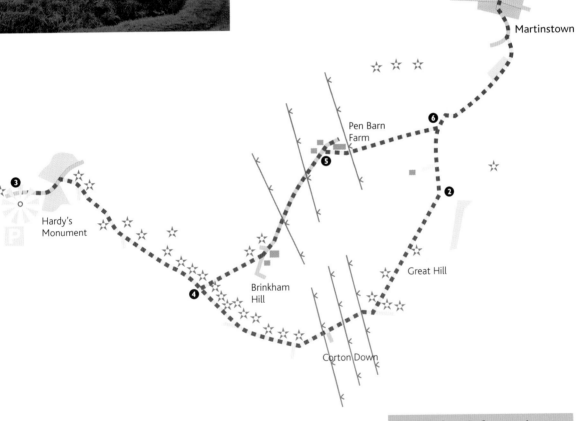

Martinstown

Pen Barn Farm

Hardy's Monument

Brinkham Hill

Great Hill

Corton Down

0   1 km   1 mile

further information

Hardy's Monument was built in 1848 to celebrate the life of Dorset's most famous maritime hero, Sir Thomas Masterman Hardy (of 'Kiss me, Hardy' fame). The monument is owned by The National Trust and is staffed from April to September. The climb to the parapet costs £1.

Difficulty rating   Time

▲ Hills or Fells, Pub, Toilets, Museum, National Trust, Wildlife, Birds, Flowers, Great Views, Butterflies, Food Shop, Tea Shop

Around Glastonbury

A short tour of the town, including optional visits to the Abbey ruins and Glastonbury Thorn, the Chalice Well and other points of religious interest, plus the obligatory pilgrimage to the Tor.

❶ From the car park in Magdalene Street turn right, passing the entrance to the Abbey. Turn right onto the High Street. Walk up the High Street, passing the tourist information office on the left (the Lake Village Museum is housed here). Continue past St John's Church. Turn right along Lambrook Street, and carry on as far as the gateway of Abbey House on the right.

❷ Turn up Dod Lane and take the driveway on the right, signed 'Footpath to Tor', to reach a squeeze stile. Follow the path uphill through fields to a lane and continue ahead.

❸ Turn left to follow Bulwarks Lane to its end. At the road (Wick Hollow), turn uphill to reach the crossroads.

❹ Take the lane to the right, with the Tor visible ahead, to reach a junction. Turn left and continue as far as the footpath to the Tor. Follow the path into a field, soon to climb to a stepped path. The path rises steeply to reach the summit and monument, where there are superb views.

❺ Descend the Tor to reach a metal gate. Take the footpath downhill to Well House Lane. Turn left, then right at the road to arrive at Chalice Well. Turn right along Chilkwell Street to reach, on the left at the junction with Bere Lane, the Somerset Rural Life Museum.

❻ Turn left onto Bere Lane, then right downhill at the crossroads to return to Magdalene Street, to visit Almshouses Chapel. Turn left and continue past the former pumphouse to return to the start of the walk.

further information

Glastonbury was the first Christian sanctuary in Britain and is the legendary burial-place of King Arthur. The abbey ruins are open every day (except Christmas Day) from 9.30 a.m. to 6 p.m. (or dusk if earlier).

Chalice Well is open every day – visiting times vary according to the season, so check beforehand if you wish to visit. The waters of the well were once considered curative.

The Somerset Rural Life Museum is open 10 a.m. to 5 p.m., Tuesday to Friday, April to October, and at weekends from 2 to 6 p.m.

The Mump, the distinctive and extraordinary mound of Glastonbury Tor, can be spotted from miles away.

access information

Glastonbury is on the A361. Park in Magdalene Street, adjacent to Glastonbury Abbey grounds.

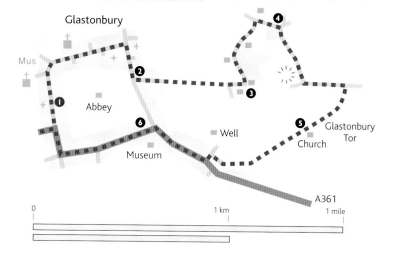

Glastonbury

Mus

Abbey

Museum

Well

Church

Glastonbury Tor

A361

0   1 km   1 mile

▲ Map: Explorer OL 45

▲ Distance: 5 km/3 miles

▲ Walk ID: 108 John Stewart

Difficulty rating

Time

▲ Hills or Fells, Great Views, Wildlife, Birds, Flowers

Beckbury Monument from Stanway

This circular walk in the heart of the Cotswolds involves a gentle climb up the escarpment to a point with a superb view. The return follows a section of the Cotswold Way.

❶ From the Stanway crossroads, take the minor road heading south to Wood Stanway. Continue on this road and take the left fork. Turn right onto the lane at the start of Wood Stanway, then turn right beyond the cottage on the right.

❷ Go through the gate and turn sharp left. Head over the meadow towards the wood. Follow the grassy track uphill, keeping the wood on the right. Where the wood ends, cross the stile and turn sharp left, continuing towards the top of a steep bank.

❸ On top of the bank is a monument and viewpoint. Just to the back of the monument go through the wooden gate towards Beckbury Camp and continue on the grassy track, with the edge of the escarpment on the left. The path soon turns sharp right following the field boundary, terminating at a stony lane. Turn left and follow the track.

❹ At the road, turn left through the wooden gate onto a grassy path. The path descends the escarpment towards Wood Stanway. After a metal gate turn

right and continue downhill, keeping the wall on your right. Follow the yellow markers over several stiles. Continue as the path meanders towards the village. At the valley bottom go through the metal gate onto the stony track. Pass the farm buildings and cottages.

❺ After the cottages turn right at the metal gate. Follow the path, keeping the field boundaries on the left until reaching a road. Turn left and continue to the start of walk.

Sheep graze in verdant, rolling countryside, in the Cotswolds near Stow-on-the-Wold.

access information

The walk starts at the Stanway crossroads on the B4077 road north-west from Stow-on-the-Wold. There is good but limited off-road parking just south of the crossroads on the minor road leading to Wood Stanway.

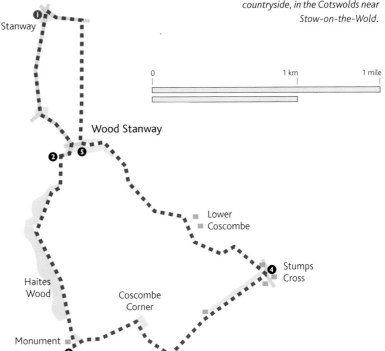

South & South-east England

The waterside walks of South and South-east England take in historic coasts, marshlands teeming with wildlife, and splendid canals. Highlights include the Saxon Shore Way and Virginia Water.

▲ Map: Explorer 163

▲ Distance: 5.64 km/3½ miles

▲ Walk ID: 873 Ian Elmes

Difficulty rating

Time

▲ River, Pub, Toilets, Castle,
Great Views, Food Shop

Hoo Marina from Lower Upnor via the Saxon Shore Way

This walk begins in the delightful village of Lower Upnor, then follows part of the Saxon Shore Way along the River Medway. The route continues into Hoo, then back across open fields to Lower Upnor.

❶ From the car park, turn right towards the Medway Yacht Club. At the gate, bear right and follow the footpath to the end. Drop down to the beach and follow the Saxon Shore Way. Follow the raised footpath at the Wilsonian Sailing Club, then continue along the beach, following the line of the river.

❷ When you reach a raised footpath, follow this to the Hoo Ness Yacht Club. Go through the gateway and follow the track ahead, bearing right just before the white gate. Follow this path until you reach a car parking area. Follow the high metal fence, then walk along the road past the Marina Office.

❸ Continue straight ahead, along a gravel track then a footpath. Out in the open, bear right, following the 'Saxon Shore' marker post. Walk past the yachts to the end of the path. By the fence, turn right to cross the road and walk between the bus depot and the steel works.

❹ Cross the road and follow the footpath left of Whitton Marina, coming out opposite a factory. Turn left along the road. Take the footpath directly ahead of you towards three distant houses. Before you reach the houses, bear left onto another path to the road.

❺ Turn left at the main road, then right on the farm track by Church Farm Lodge. Follow the track up the hill. Go through the gate at the top. At the crossroads, go straight on, following the track to an enclosed footpath past some houses.

❻ Turn left and follow the road up the hill. At the top, follow the enclosed footpath straight ahead. Ignoring the footpath to the right, carry straight on, following the footpath down towards the river, bearing left at the yellow marker post. At the bottom, follow the road back to the car park.

access information

Lower Upnor lies just off the A228 north of Rochester. The walk starts at the car park.

further information

The village of Lower Upnor is ideal for spending relaxed evenings, with two pubs, great views across to Chatham Historic Dockyard, and a steady stream of yachts going up and down the river. Nearby Upper Upnor also has two pubs and a castle.

A scene of peace and tranquillity is often the reward when taking this riverside walk.

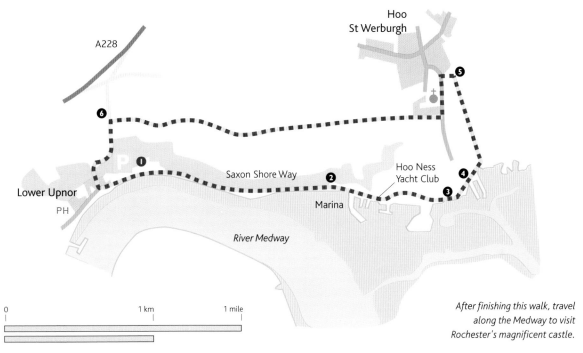

Hoo
St Werburgh

A228

⑤

⑥

Lower Upnor

P ①

PH

Saxon Shore Way

②

Hoo Ness
Yacht Club

④

③

Marina

River Medway

0   1 km   1 mile

*After finishing this walk, travel
along the Medway to visit
Rochester's magnificent castle.*

▲ Map: Explorer 145

▲ Distance: 15 km/9¼ miles

▲ Walk ID: 667 Barrie England

Difficulty rating

Time

●●●◖

▲ Lake, Pub, Birds, Great Views

Basingstoke Canal and Surrounding Countryside

access information

Winchfield is on the B3016 south of the M3, off the A30 between Basingstoke and Camberley. The walk starts at the Barley Mow pub. Parking is available at the canal bridge.

Beginning and ending at Winchfield's Barley Mow pub, this walk follows part of the Basingstoke Canal and crosses open countryside. The stretch at Step 6 can be difficult after heavy rain, so an alternative is given in the 'further information'.

❶ From the car park, turn left and follow the canal, walking under Blacksmith's Bridge and Double Bridge. Immediately before Chequers Bridge turn left, walk through Crookham Wharf car park, cross the road carefully and turn left, facing the oncoming traffic.

❷ Turn left into Stroud Lane. After Willow Cottage, turn left and cross a stream and a stile. Cross the field diagonally left. Cross another stile. Follow the path up across the field, between the pylon and the woods, then down into woodland and across a stream to join a track.

❸ Follow the track between the houses. Turn left over a stile and follow the signposted path across the field to two stiles among trees, then onto a track. Continue over another stile. Follow the narrow path between two fences. Cross a left-hand stile into a field and head to the right of a pylon. Follow the path to the road.

❹ Cross over and follow the path opposite, beside Double Bridge Farm. Cross a stile and follow the track over Blacksmith's Bridge and down to climb another stile. Turn right, then left to walk beside Tundry Pond. At the bridge, bear left. Cross a stile and after a short distance cross another stile on the right.

❺ Fork left and follow the path up across a field towards the barn on the horizon. Follow a track past the barn to the summit, then down past woods and Dogmersfield Lake on the right. Go slightly uphill and across another track to reach two lodges.

❻ Turn right immediately after the lodges and follow the path through the woods to the canal. Turn left and follow the path to turn right across the canal bridge. Turn right again and down to follow the canal all the way back to Barley Mow Bridge. Walk under it and turn left to the car park.

further information

After heavy rain, at Step 6 continue walking to the main A287. Turn right and walk with great care on the right side of the road. After 750 m take the first right at the roundabout and follow this narrow road through Broad Oak to the bridge over the canal.

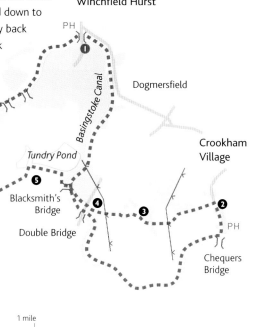

▲ Map: Explorer 121

▲ Distance: 7 km/4¼ miles

▲ Walk ID: 76 Nicholas Rudd-Jones

Difficulty rating

Time

River, Pub, Church, Wildlife, Great Views

Arundel Castle.

Houghton and River Arun

This is a circular walk around the River Arun, taking in the delightful villages of North Stoke and South Stoke on the Sussex Downs above Arundel. If you have time, you can take a detour into Arundel Park.

❶ From the small road next to the phone box and post box, take a footpath to the right. Climb two stiles, cross a track and continue on the grassy path downhill. At the bottom of the field, the path becomes gravelled. Cross the footbridge and follow the path as it swings right. Climb the stile and turn left at the river.

❷ Climb the next stile to turn right and cross the bridge. Follow the track past the houses and St Leonard's Church in South Stoke. Join the road and swing left past the barn on the right. Turn right off the road and follow the bridleway behind the barn.

❸ At the next bridleway signpost, turn left to follow the stony track. Go through a gate and turn right to follow the path around the field edge. Pass the gate back into the woods. Continue past a metal gate leading into Arundel Park on the left. Follow the path along the river, passing under white cliffs.

❹ Go through a metal gate at the end of the path and follow the road uphill into Houghton village. At the crossroads, cross the B2139 and follow the minor road signposted to Bury across the fields.

❺ Turn right when the South Downs Way crosses the road. At the river, follow the path round to the right to Amberley Bridge. Turn left over the bridge and take the footpath halfway across the bridge on the right, heading towards North Stoke.

❻ Cross a subsidiary bridge, then turn right, back alongside the river. Climb a stile and shortly afterwards take the path to the left. On reaching the North Stoke Road, turn right and return to the start.

further information

The River Arun is tidal and very prone to flooding, so it is a good idea to check the condition before you start out. At Step 4, there is a path alongside the river straight to Houghton Bridge, which can be used to shorten the route in dry weather.

access information

North Stoke lies south of Amberley Station, off the B2139 from Storrington. Parking is available near the phone box in North Stoke. You can also take a train to Amberley (on the Pulborough line from London) and start the walk from there.

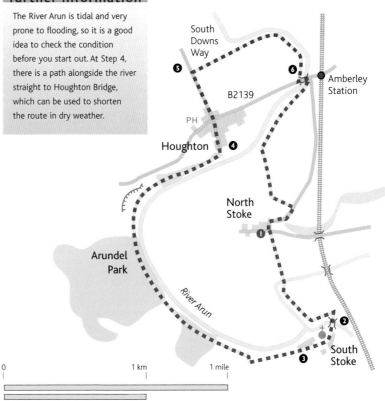

▲ Map: Explorer 15

▲ Distance: 12 km/7½ miles

▲ Walk ID: 2078 David Stewart

Difficulty rating

Time

▲ Sea, Pub, Toilets, Play Area, National Trust/NTS, Birds, Great Views, Butterflies, Café, Good for Kids

Osmington and Ringstead

This is an enjoyable, family-friendly walk covering a delightful stretch of the Dorset coast and surrounding countryside.

1 Come out through the car park entrance and walk back along the road for about 1 km. Take the footpath on the right and walk downhill. Follow the track through the farm and uphill again until you emerge at the A352.

2 Cross the road to the footpath directly opposite and proceed uphill. Further on the path crosses a field and is harder to follow – head to the left of the mobile phone mast. Pass through the gate at the bottom and cross the track from Poxwell Manor (on your right). Walk up towards the mast, following the sign for the Hardy Way. Once at the mast, veer to the left and follow the ancient trackway to White Horse Hill.

3 Just short of the summit and the gated stile, there is a left turn signposted to Osmington. Follow this stony track downhill to the village. Turn round on your way down to admire the White Horse on the hillside behind you.

4 At Osmington, turn left onto Village Street, which is signposted to Osmington Mills. The street bends sharply to the right before joining the main road at the Sun Ray pub. Turn left onto the road and walk for about 125 m before crossing. Proceed along the footpath by the cottage. When you reach the stile by the busy dairy farm, cross over and go through the gate opposite. (If the farmer is moving cattle

the path may appear barred.) Follow the path as it veers to the left until you emerge into an open field.

5 Make your way to the field boundary by the campsite. Follow the hedge to the far corner and climb the stile to join the coast path. Walk along the boards through the trees to the quiet road. Turn right and walk for a couple of hundred metres to the Smuggler's Inn.

6 Walk round the left-hand side of the pub to find the coastal path. Pass through the kissing gate by the white house and then on up to the next kissing gate to follow the coastal path to Ringstead, where the path veers inland.

The White Horse, cut into the turf to reveal the chalk, at White Horse Hill.

access information

The walk begins at the South Down car park at Ringstead, just off the A352 east of Weymouth.

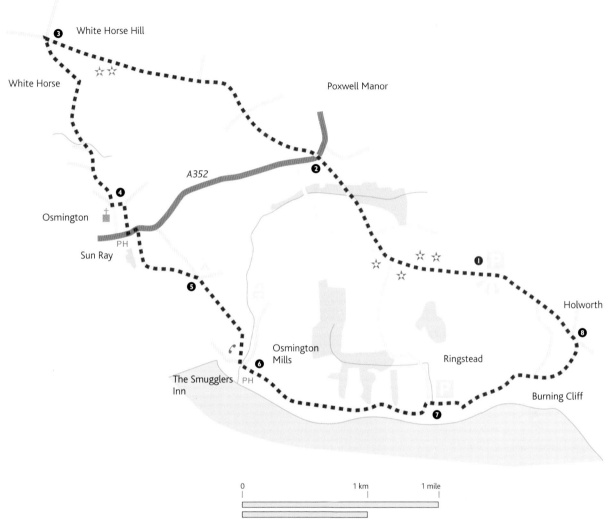

White Horse Hill

White Horse

Poxwell Manor

A352

Osmington

Sun Ray

Osmington Mills

Ringstead

Holworth

The Smugglers Inn

Burning Cliff

0   1 km   1 mile

7 As you come up to the car park, take the right-hand turn for the coastal path, signposted to White Nothe. After a while, cross the stile on the right, walk through the meadow to the beach and walk along to the steps, at the top of which you rejoin the coastal path at Burning Cliff. Continue on the coastal path to Holworth, climbing steadily and veering left.

8 Where the track forks, keep to the left and head back to your car.

further information

This is a child-friendly section of coast, with few dangers and an opportunity to spend time on the beach.

There are toilets, a beach shop and refreshment facilities at Ringstead.

The Smuggler's Inn serves food and has a children's play area.

▲ Map: Explorer 160
▲ Distance: 8.86 km/5½ miles
▲ Walk ID: 736 Tony Brotherton

Difficulty rating

Time

▲ Lake, Pub, Toilets, Wildlife, Birds, Flowers, Great Views

Around Virginia Water

This walk around Virginia Water, in Windsor Great Park, has some stunning vistas. The Valley Gardens are among the world's best woodland gardens. Detours from the main route given here will reveal many interesting features and landmarks.

❶ From Blacknest car park, walk ahead on the broad woodland path to reach the lake opposite the stone bridge. Turn right to follow the lakeside path, eventually passing the 'ruins' to your right. Walk on to the cascade, and continue downhill.

❷ Cross the stone bridge and look out for the 'hidden' path between the rhododendrons on the left. Climb a short path to rejoin the lakeside path and walk past the Wheatsheaf car park. Carry on alongside the lake to the totem-pole. From here, take the sand and gravel path uphill towards Valley Gardens.

❸ Near the top of the gardens, turn right to reach a signpost at a cross-paths. Follow the 'Savill Gardens' sign through parkland to a five-fingered signpost. Take the path to Obelisk Pond. Follow the path around the pond, then continue to cross a balustraded bridge.

❹ When the path gives way to grass, bear half-left between trees to follow the edge of a wood on your left. Heading towards the equestrian statue, reach the crossroads at the corner of Smith's Lawn. Turn left, and follow the rail fence, with the grandstand ahead.

❺ Go left at the 'Guards Polo Club' sign. Bear right to re-enter Valley Gardens and continue to the heather garden entrance. Go into the heather garden and bear left along the broad grass path. Leave the

garden through either of two gates, taking the path to the right back to the five-fingered signpost. Follow the sandy path half-right into woods, then a broad grassy swathe back to the lake path.

❻ Follow the lake path, finally turning left to join the road between the main lake and Johnson's Pond. Leave the road to walk alongside the horse gallop, then rejoin the road to cross the stone bridge. Bear left on the path back to the lakeside. Go ahead on the woodland path to Blacknest car park, or turn left for the Wheatsheaf car park.

further information

There are no stiles, brambles or nettles on this walk – just a few gentle slopes, rhododendrons, azaleas and magnolias in spring, and a fantastic variety of birdlife both on and around the lake. Look out for green woodpeckers, kingfishers, herons and great crested grebes, as well as exotic ducks and geese.

Enjoy the abundant floral delights in the peaceful surroundings of Virginia Water.

access information

The route passes close to the three main car parks that serve the park. They are at Blacknest (current charge £1.50), Wheatsheaf (current charge £3.50) and Savill Gardens (current charge £2.00). There is free verge car parking at Mill Lane. Wheatsheaf car park is accessible by buses between Bagshot and Egham.

Visit the nearby Windsor Castle, the splendid royal residence of Queen Elizabeth II.

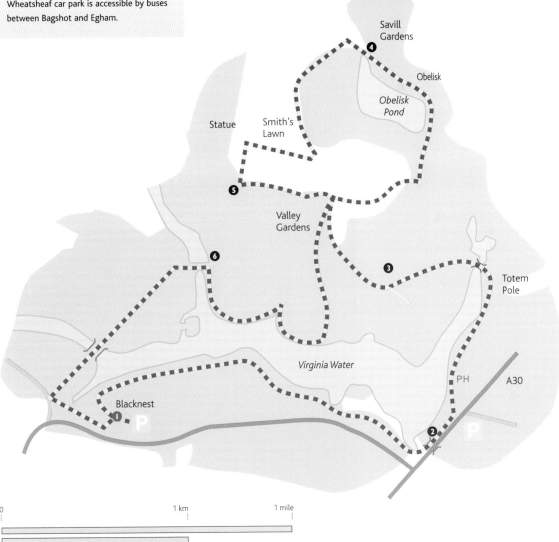

▲ Map: Explorer 192

▲ Distance: 8.05 km/5 miles

▲ Walk ID: 1183 Brian and Anne Sandland

Difficulty rating

Time

Pub, Toilets, Church, Wildlife, Birds, Flowers, Butterflies, Great Views, Industrial Archaeology

The Grand Union Canal and Great Brickhill from Three Locks Inn

From the Three Locks Inn, this walk follows the towpath of the Grand Union Canal, then crosses fields to Great Brickhill village on a ridge with great views. From here, the route follows a bridleway to rejoin the towpath and return to the start point.

1 From the car park, cross the road and go down to the canal towpath. Follow the path to the first bridge, then cross the canal and continue on the opposite bank. Pass the lock at Stoke Hammond and carry on under the bridge. Continue for some distance to the next bridge. Look for an exit to the right and climb the steps to the road.

2 Turn right and follow the road. Cross the river bridges, then Lower Rectory Farm on your right. Opposite the entrance to Westfield Farm on your left, turn right onto a signposted path. Go through the metal gate and follow the broad path diagonally left across the field, then bear right to follow trees and a hedge on your left. Cross a fence and bear left.

3 Follow an old wall on your left, cross a stile by a metal gate, then head for the further of two Scots pines to reach another gate just after a yellow way-mark. Beyond the gate, follow a track between hedges. Go through another gate and turn left onto the tarmacked lane, past Great Brickhill Church. At the T-junction, turn right into Lower Way.

The Grand Union Canal is a modern man-made wonder and is enjoyed today for a variety of leisure activities.

access information

The Three Locks car park and picnic site is on the east side of the A4146 between Bletchley and Leighton Buzzard.

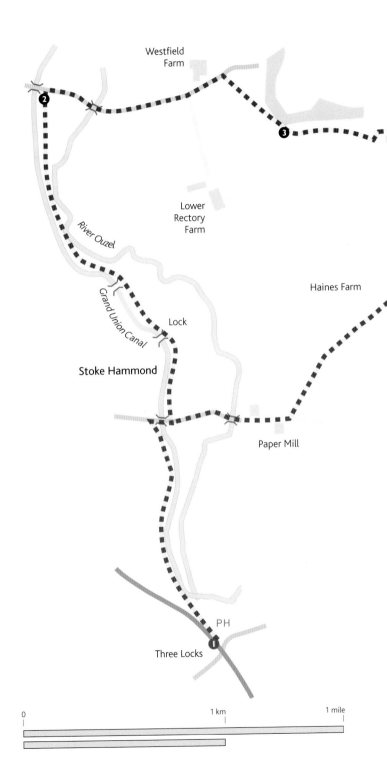

Westfield
Farm

2

Lower
Rectory
Farm

River Ouzel

Grand Union Canal

Lock

Stoke Hammond

3

Great
Brickhill

PH

Haines Farm

4

5

Paper Mill

1

PH

Three Locks

0   1 km   1 mile

further information

Once you are up on the ridge at Great
Brickhill, you will have the opportunity to
extend the walk in a number of ways, one
of which is to follow the Greensand Ridge
Path over the ridge, turning right above
Bragenham to follow a path back to the
T-junction at Step 5.

4 Follow this road through the village.
Pass the Old Red Lion Inn on your right,
then take a concrete lane which slopes
down to the right opposite Cromwell
Cottages. Continue past Broomhill
House on your left and Green Farm on
your right, then when the road goes
right to Haines Farm, take the broad
signposted track to the left.

5 Carry on down this track. At a T-
junction opposite the entrance to Paper
Mill farmyard, turn right. Follow this
track, crossing a river bridge, to reach
the canal bridge. Turn left back onto the
towpath and return to the start.

Woodland & Hillside

The woodland and hillside walks of South and South-east England reveal downland and deer parks, ancient battlegrounds and eerie monuments. Highlights include Avebury Ring and the 1066 Walk.

▲ Map: Explorer 157
▲ Distance: 8.5 km/5¼ miles
▲ Walk ID: 68 David Stewart

Difficulty rating

👣👣

Time

●●●

Pub, Museum, National Trust/NTS, Gift Shop, Restaurant, Great Views

The Sanctuary, West Kennet Long Barrow and Silbury Hill from Avebury

From the Avebury stone circle, this walk goes along the Stone Avenue and up to the Ridgeway with its views of 'hedgehogs' and curious burial mounds. The route then visits The Sanctuary, the West Kennet Long Barrow and Silbury Hill burial ground.

❶ From the car park, follow the signs to Avebury village. At the road, turn right into the ring. Follow the ring round to the left. Cross the main road into the next part of the ring. Bear right and climb up onto the bank. Go down the other side towards a gate. Cross the road into the field. Walk down Stone Avenue between the stones.

❷ At the end of Stone Avenue go through a gate, cross the road, and follow the path opposite. Keeping on the same side of the hedge, cross into the next field. Follow the left-hand field edge slightly uphill to the next field boundary.

❸ Turn right on the track leading towards the 'hedgehogs', a clump of trees on the horizon. Follow the path as it bears left after the hedgehogs, then turn right and follow the Ridgeway down to cross the main road.

❹ Visit The Sanctuary on the right, then follow the path signed 'Byway', directly opposite the end of the Ridgeway. Just before the path turns left and crosses a bridge, turn right and follow the path alongside the river to a road.

access information

Avebury lies halfway between Marlborough and Calne, just off the A4. The National Trust provides a free car park just before reaching Avebury village on the A4361. Buses are available from Devizes, Marlborough and Swindon (Wiltshire Bus Line, 0845 7090899).

A fine aerial view of Avebury village. Strong shadows throw the ancient stone circle into relief.

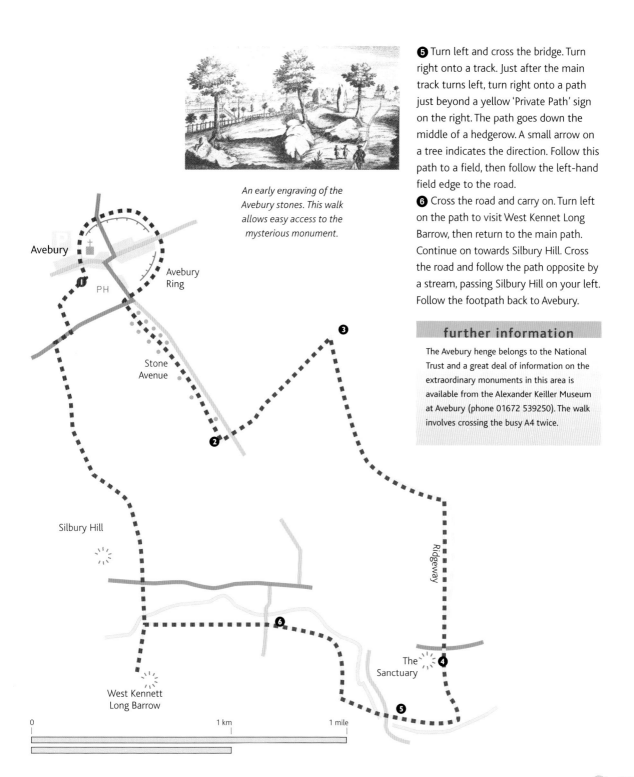

An early engraving of the Avebury stones. This walk allows easy access to the mysterious monument.

5 Turn left and cross the bridge. Turn right onto a track. Just after the main track turns left, turn right onto a path just beyond a yellow 'Private Path' sign on the right. The path goes down the middle of a hedgerow. A small arrow on a tree indicates the direction. Follow this path to a field, then follow the left-hand field edge to the road.

6 Cross the road and carry on. Turn left on the path to visit West Kennet Long Barrow, then return to the main path. Continue on towards Silbury Hill. Cross the road and follow the path opposite by a stream, passing Silbury Hill on your left. Follow the footpath back to Avebury.

further information

The Avebury henge belongs to the National Trust and a great deal of information on the extraordinary monuments in this area is available from the Alexander Keiller Museum at Avebury (phone 01672 539250). The walk involves crossing the busy A4 twice.

Avebury

Avebury Ring

PH

Stone Avenue

Silbury Hill

Ridgeway

The Sanctuary

West Kennett Long Barrow

0   1 km   1 mile

▲ Map: Explorer OL 29

▲ Distance: 8 km/5 miles

▲ Walk ID: 546 David L. White

Difficulty rating

Time

▲ Hills, Sea, Pub, Toilets, Church, Wildlife, Birds, Flowers, Great Views

Niton and St Catherine's Down from Blackgang

This walk is in an area with a seafaring history, with three lighthouses from different periods and a smuggling tradition around Blackgang and Niton. Blackgang now clings precariously to the cliff-edge, slowly disappearing as the cliff erodes.

1 From the seaward side of the car park, climb up some steps and follow the path to the cliff top. Turn left towards Niton and follow the path past the radio mast station. After the second stile beyond the radio station, turn immediately left over another stile, heading inland.

The southern coastline of the Isle of Wight with Blackgang and most of the walk area visible.

2 Keeping the fence on your right, walk across the field to a stile at the far side. Cross a small meadow, bearing slightly left, to climb another stile. Walk through a coppice path to the main road. Follow the road to the right until it bears left, marked 'Through traffic', to the church. At the lychgate, turn left and go up Pan Lane. When the lane becomes a bridle path, carry on, turning left at a junction of paths.

access information

Blackgang lies just off the southern tip of the Isle of Wight, off the A3055. There is a large car park. The nearest bus stop is Blackgang. If you are travelling by ferry from the mainland, the best crossings are the Portsmouth/Ryde catamaran, the Southsea/Ryde hovercraft and the Portsmouth/Fishbourne car ferry.

3 Go through a metal gate and follow a blue arrow straight ahead. Go through another metal gate at the far side of the field. (At this point you can turn right and walk across the field, bearing slightly right towards a signpost, then follow a bridleway to Hoy's Monument. Return to the gate to continue the walk at Step 4.)

4 Turn immediately left and climb to the summit of the hill, where the Old Oratory stands, for fantastic views. The Old Oratory was one of the original lighthouses, built in 1314. From the Old Oratory, cross the field, heading towards the sea, to climb a stile. Follow the path down to the start of the walk.

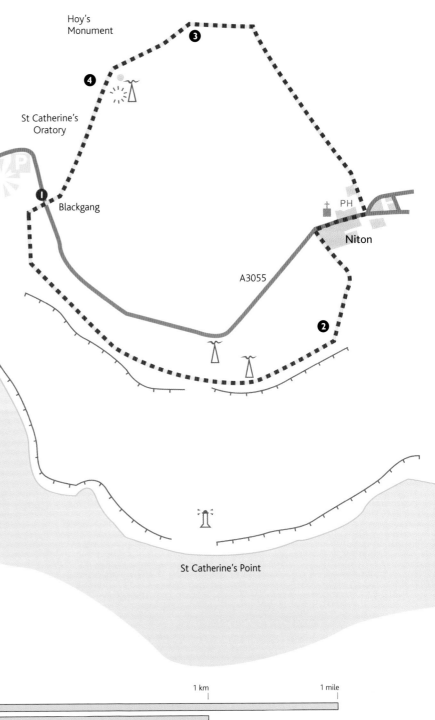

further information

A Heritage Coast information board in the car park tells you about the area. Points of interest include St Catherine's Lighthouse, which houses the Niton radio station, and Hoy's Monument, which commemorates Czar Alexander I's visit to England and also honours British soldiers who fell during the Crimean War.

▲ Map: Explorer 123
▲ Distance: 6.44 km/4 miles
▲ Walk ID: 590 Martin Heaps

Difficulty rating

Time

▲ Sea, Pub, Toilets, National
Trust/NTS, Great Views

East Dean Round

This is an easy walk on grassy downland paths and farm tracks. There are wonderful views from the start of the walk over Eastbourne and further east towards Pevensey Marshes and Hastings, and later from Went Hill.

❶ From the bus stop, follow the well-defined grassy path, which starts nearby, towards the sea. When the triangulation point comes into view with the dew pond near by, bear right towards the road and keep to the right.

❷ Cross the road carefully and go through the gate on the far side. Follow the path, which can get muddy, past Crapham Down and into East Hale Bottom, passing a pumping station. Walk on through the next gate and past a group of farm buildings to join a concrete track at Cornish Farm.

❸ Follow the track round to the left, heading towards Belle Tout, a disused lighthouse now converted to a residential home. When you reach the road, cross over to join the path and turn right towards Birling Gap.

❹ When the road alongside turns almost back on itself to the right, walk on through the car park towards the toilet block, and turn left onto the stony track. Follow the track as it bears right up Went Hill.

❺ Where the path forks left, turn right downhill towards East Dean. The path bears right to a gate, then passes several houses and becomes a narrow road. The road emerges on the village green.

❻ Facing the Tiger Inn, walk to the left and onto the main road. At the road, turn right and then left when you reach Downsview Lane. This track runs parallel to the road through the golf course and back to the start of the walk.

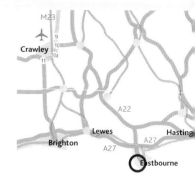

access information

The start and end point is easily accessible from Eastbourne town centre, with a bus stop only a short distance away.

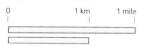

further information

The energetic can access the start point from the town centre along the A259 towards Brighton. The climb up East Dean Hill can be somewhat taxing, but is certainly rewarding for the views.

Glimpses of the evocative chalk hills of the South Downs are to be enjoyed on the coastal part of the journey.

▲ Map: Explorer 121

▲ Distance: 8.5 km/5¼ miles

▲ Walk ID: 75 Nicholas Rudd-Jones

Difficulty rating

Time

▲ Hills, Pub, Church, National Trust/NTS, Wildlife, Birds, Great Views, Woodland

The Sussex Downs.

Sutton, Barlavington and South Downs Way

A3

A272

Billingshurst

Midhurst

A29

A285

A283

A27

A285

Brighton

Chichester

Bognor Regis

This varied walk climbs to the top of the South Downs, where there are great views of the Downs and the south coast. Much of the walk follows lovely woodland paths.

❶ From the car park, walk up through the gate and alongside the stone wall. Turn right through the gate, climb the stone steps and turn right behind the building. Cross the garden to the kissing gate. Cross the field diagonally left to the far edge. Follow the grassy path straight ahead. At the meadow corner, walk straight ahead though the woods.

❷ Cross a stream and a stile. Turn right towards a gate. Climb a stile and turn left to Barlavington. Turn left along the track. Go through gates into the churchyard and out at the far side. Follow the road round to the left. At the junction, follow the bridleway uphill and into the woods, swinging left. At a small bench, follow the chalky right-hand path. Leave the woods and turn left.

❸ At the crossroads, follow the path uphill across the field. Go through the gate, the woods and another gate, then between fields to more woods. At the next junction, turn right uphill, then immediately left uphill. At the blue waymark, join the track uphill to the left. Keep left, following the National Trust sign to the Bignor Hill car park. Walk downhill past the 'Roman Villa' sign.

❹ Turn left on a steep signposted footpath. Later, join a track to the right then immediately turn left, leaving the woods. Follow the field edge, climb a stile, and cross the fields. Ignore a yellow waymarked stile and swing right along the track into woods. Pass a house on your left and at the road turn left to walk into Bignor.

❺ Go through the gate to the left of the next house and follow the path into woods. Cross a footbridge. Follow the path to another footbridge. Bear right at the footpath sign. Cross a footbridge and a stile. Head for the footpath sign across the meadow then uphill to a stile. Cross the field to Sutton. Follow the path between trees back to the pub.

access information

Sutton lies between the A285 Petworth to Chichester road and the A29 Pulborough to Bognor Regis road. Parking is available at the White Horse Pub in Sutton (patrons only, so if you park here it is necessary to patronize at some point).

further information

There is much evidence of the area's long history along this route, which passes several tumuli and a Neolithic camp. At Bignor, there are the remains of a Roman villa. The raised bank crossing the track at Step 3 is Stane Street, a Roman road.

Barlavington

❷

PH

Sutton

❶

Barlavington Down

❸

Roman Villa

❺

Farm Hill

Bignor

Bignor Hill

❹

0   1 km   1 mile

▲ Map: Explorer 124

▲ Distance: 8.5 km/5¼ miles

▲ Walk ID: 206 Jacky Rix-Brown

Difficulty rating

Time

River, Sea, Toilets, Museum, Church, Castle, Wildlife, Birds, Flowers, Great Views

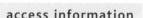

1066 Walk – Battle to Bexhill

This spur of the 1066 Walk from Pevensey to Rye via Battle takes you from Battle to Bexhill-on-Sea. It starts at Battle Abbey and heads south through rolling hills, the Fore Wood Nature Reserve and the village of Crowhurst on the way to Bexhill.

❶ From the Abbey, walk past the Pilgrim's Rest restaurant. At the track, follow the 1066 walk symbol. When the track divides, fork left to Bexhill, past the wood, over a hill and across a stream. Carry on, crossing a tarmacked track, and climb a stile to follow the path parallel to a road.

❷ Climb the stile and cross the road carefully to Talham Lane opposite. Fork right to Peppering Eye Farm and follow the path straight ahead up the hill.
At the junction of paths near a cottage, fork left through the woods, following the 1066 symbol. Turn left downhill with the footpath. Cross the stream into another wood.

❸ Bend right on the main track and follow it through the wood. Just past a pond on the left, fork right to the stile at the edge of the wood. Follow the 1066 symbol across the field, bear left up the hill and continue to the road.

❹ Turn right to Crowhurst. Turn right, past the church, down the hill and follow the road through the village (keeping left at fork). Where the road bends sharp left, turn right over a stile to follow the footpath beside a stream.

❺ Just past Adam's Farm, follow the 1066 sign to the right. Follow the zigzag path to cross two bridges, then continue across the marshland to climb an inconspicuous stile. Continue beside the hedge, then across the field, converging with the railway embankment. Cross the disused railway. Follow the track past Little Worsham Farm. Turn right at the T-junction, then left at another junction to Upper Worsham Farm.

❻ Where the tracks fork, climb a stile in between and follow the path, crossing a stream, to reach the A2036. Cross to follow a footpath between gardens to a road. Following the 1066 signs, turn left to the next junction, then right along a road leading to a footpath and bridge which crosses the A259 and continues to a road leading to the car park.

Battle
Battle Abbey
❶
Hastings 1066
❷
Peppering Eye Farm
❸
❹
PH
Crowhurst
❺ Adam's Farm
Worsham Farm
Disused railway
A2036
Bexhill
A259
❻

further information

The 1066 walk commemorates the Battle of Hastings, where William the Conqueror famously defeated King Harold on Senlac Hill. There are plenty of places of interest to visit along the walk, including Battle Abbey, the ancient church and centuries-old yew tree in Crowhurst, and the museum and ruins of a manor in Bexhill.

Battle Abbey was built on the site of the defining battle between William the Conqueror and King Harold.

0   1 km   1 mile

Peaceful now, this is the site of the Battle of Hastings, 1066, near the historic town of Battle in East Sussex.

▲ Map: Explorer 180
▲ Distance: 8.45 km/5¼ miles
▲ Walk ID: 1234 Ron and Jenny Glynn

Difficulty rating

Time

▲ Lake, Church, Stately Home, Wildlife, Birds, Flowers, Great Views, Butterflies, Woodland

Wotton Underwood from Ludgershall

This gentle walk begins in Ludgershall and wanders through Buckinghamshire on a mixture of footpaths, bridleways and quiet country roads. The route passes through the beautiful parkland surrounding the magnificent Wotton House.

❶ Take the minor road, just before the church at Peartree Farm, signed to Wotton, and walk along to the junction. Walk over to the narrow path at Wotton End, and follow the hedge line to cross a brook. Fork right over common ground to an opening.

❷ Walk past the stile on the left at a junction of paths, and follow the left-hand hedge in ridge and furrow meadowland. Climb a stile and cross the next two fields, with woodland over to the left. Cross a double stile and footbridge. Turn right on a bridleway, with the hedge on your right. Go through a walkers' gate and then another gate.

❸ Cross the road and another stile. Cross a large field, with farm buildings on your right, gradually climbing uphill. Head slightly right over two stiles. Climb a stile in the corner of the field to a hard track. Walk over and cross the stile to the left of the white gate to Middle Farm. Follow the field edge until you reach a metal kissing gate.

❹ Turn right through a wooden gate and pass the back of a farmhouse to a hard path, passing through a wild flower meadow and crossing a miniature railway track. Pass a red-brick house, then turn right through a gate to walk by Wotton House. The path runs downhill.

❺ Walk ahead over a large green to join the road, and follow it along between trees and hedgerows. Turn right past Lawn Farm. Just before the railway, fork right towards Ludgershall and Kingswood on a narrow road through woodland.

❻ At the junction at the end of the woodland, follow the lane ahead to Ludgershall. Turn left into Church Lane, and retrace your steps to the start.

After Middle Farm the walk passes the grandiose Wotton House, in Wotton Underwood, seen here with the 'ha-ha' in the foreground.

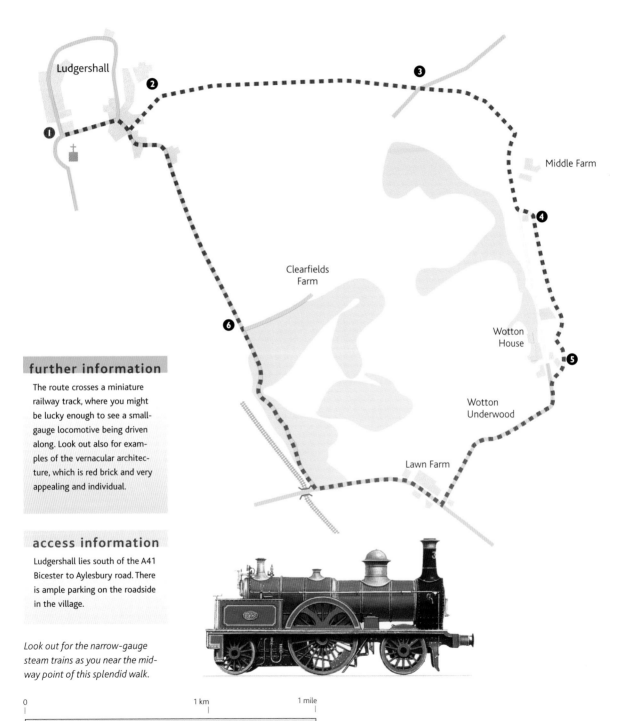

Ludgershall

❶ ❷ ❸

Middle Farm

❹

Clearfields
Farm

❻

Wotton
House

❺

Wotton
Underwood

Lawn Farm

further information

The route crosses a miniature
railway track, where you might
be lucky enough to see a small-
gauge locomotive being driven
along. Look out also for examples of the vernacular architecture, which is red brick and very
appealing and individual.

access information

Ludgershall lies south of the A41
Bicester to Aylesbury road. There
is ample parking on the roadside
in the village.

*Look out for the narrow-gauge
steam trains as you near the midway point of this splendid walk.*

0   1 km   1 mile

Central England

Coastal & Waterside

The waterside walks of Central England embrace Norfolk's shores and marshes, Cambridgeshire fens and Oxford's tow-paths. Highlights include Ludham Marshes, Houghton Mill and Calcutt Locks.

▲ Map: Explorer OL 40

▲ Distance: 5.5 km/3½ miles

▲ Walk ID: 800 Stephanie Kedik

Difficulty rating

Time

▲ River, Pub, Toilets, Play Area, Church, Wildlife, Birds, Flowers, Butterflies, Gift Shop, Food Shop, Good for Kids, Nature Trail, Tea Shop

Ludham Marshes

access information

Ludham can be reached by car from Norwich (A1151/A1062) or by bus (for information, phone Norfolk Bus Information on 0845 300 6116 or Traveline on 0870 6082608).

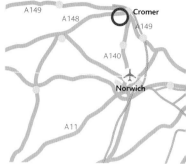

This picturesque stroll starts in the beautiful village of Ludham and takes in Ludham Marshes Nature Reserve. Renowned for their abundance of wildlife, the marshes sit alongside the River Thurne, where boatyards are dotted along the banks.

❶ From the centre of Ludham, take the main Yarmouth Road past the Ludham village sign at Bakers Arms Green. Further down, on the right, is a little path leading off and running alongside the road. Follow this until you reach a right turn where Horse Fen Road meets the Yarmouth Road.

❷ Turn right into Horse Fen Road. Continue along the lane, past Womack Water boat hire and camp site. Follow the public bridleway down to Ludham Marshes National Nature Reserve.

❸ As you take the path round the corner and into the reserve, you will pass first a garden and then a wood on your left beyond the drainage ditch (deer are sometimes seen in the wood). On your right, the marshes stretch out across to the River Thurne. Follow the footpath through the reserve.

❹ Where you meet the gravel track, take a turn to the right through the gate (which is signed 'Danger – Unstable road!'). Continue along this track and go through another gate.

❺ When you reach Horse Fen pumping station, turn right to follow the green footpath sign. Across the bridge, follow the footpath along the river, keeping the river on your left. Although this stretch can be a bit overgrown in summer, it is compensated by the views of the river.

❻ Follow the footpath back from the river, up the creek, and out of the reserve at the side of Hunters Yard. Walk back up Horse Fen Road, past Womack Water and the boatyard. At the top of Horse Fen Road, turn left and follow the road leading back into Ludham village.

The marshes are renowned for their wildlife and provide a peaceful environment for sailors of small craft.

further information

In the summer months Ludham Marshes Nature Reserve buzzes with insects and butterflies, and there are many varieties of birds to be seen all year round. Deer are also sometimes spotted in the nearby wood. The undergrowth along the riverbank can grow quite high, so leg-covering is recommended. Boats can be hired by the day from the marina in the village.

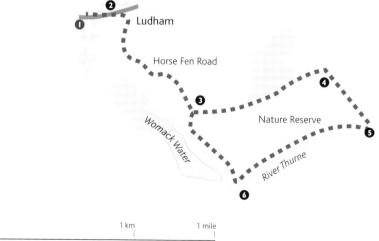

▲ Map: Explorer 23

▲ Distance: 8.86 km/5½ miles

▲ Walk ID: 810 J. and C. Boldero

Difficulty rating

Time

▲ Sea, Pub, Toilets, Churches, Roman Fort, Wildlife, Birds, Flowers, Great Views, Butterflies

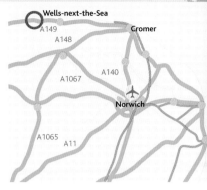

St Mary's Church, Burnham Deepdale.

Burnham Deepdale

This circular walk takes in part of the North Norfolk Coastal Path, passing tidal creeks with mussel beds and a wide variety of wading and sea birds. The return route passes the site of a 3rd-century Roman fort, then crosses Barrow Common.

❶ Starting with the garage on your left, walk along the road for a very short distance, then turn right along a 'No Through Road'. Follow the signed footpath that runs between the trees. When you reach the finger signpost, turn left along the coastal path, with the creeks on your right. Follow this winding path to the end at Brancaster Staithe, where you pass between brick sheds by a cottage.

❷ Turn left along the track, then almost immediately right, following the yellow arrow on the wall. Go along a narrow path between a fence and a brick wall, then through a gate. Follow the board walk to the end at Brancaster.

❸ Turn left along a country lane, then at the main road turn left again by the church, with the Ship Inn opposite. Turn left along London Road, then right along the narrow lane just before the last house on the right (if you reach a footpath, you have gone too far). At the end of the lane, turn right along the gravel path, then left along a country lane, following the path round the site of the Roman fort.

❹ When you reach the main road, cross it and turn left along the pavement, which is hidden between the grass and the hedge. Almost immediately, turn right up a wide, hedged track, and at the top turn right again along a grassy track.

❺ Go through the gate onto Barrow Common, ignoring the path on the left. When you reach the open space, keep to the right-hand path, which later veers left with the wood on the right. At the country lane, turn right for a very short distance, then left along another country lane. At the T-junction in Burnham Deepdale, turn right to the lay-by and the start of the walk.

access information

There is a coastal bus route (for more information, phone 0845 3006116 or Traveline on 0870 6082608). There is parking in the long lay-by opposite the garage and by the church at Burnham Deepdale, which is situated on the A149, 11.25 km west of Wells-next-the-Sea in North Norfolk.

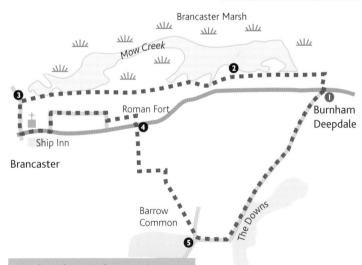

further information

Burnham Deepdale Church has an Anglo-Saxon tower and a font with a Norman bowl. At St Mary's in Brancaster, look out for a carving of a man with his head at a very strange angle. Brancaster Staithe has been a fishing port since Roman times.

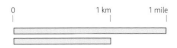

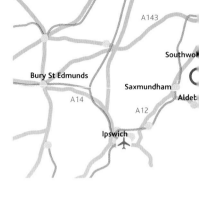

▲ Map: Explorer 212

▲ Distance: 14.49 km/9 miles

▲ Walk ID: 641 B. and A. Sandland

Difficulty rating

👣👣👣

Time

●●●●

▲ Pub, Toilets, Play Area, National Trust/NTS, Wildlife, Birds, Flowers, Great Views, Accessible for Wheelchairs

Sizewell and Minsmere from Dunwich

This walk from Dunwich crosses heath and woodland, passing through Eastbridge before taking in the majestic forest of Sizewell Belts. An alternative is to visit the dazzling dome of the Sizewell Power Station, before returning via the seashore.

❶ From the car park, go through the gap between the pine trees to the right of the toilets. Follow this wide track left over the heath (do not take the track that rises to the right). Continue until you enter woodland at a stile.

❷ Climb the stile and continue in the same direction. At a T-junction of tracks, turn left. When you reach a narrow road, cross straight over and carry on, with fields to both sides of the track.

❸ Enter more woodland and descend to meet another narrow road on a bend. Go straight ahead along the road, bearing left at a house. Cross the bridge over the Minsmere, and keep going, passing the Eel's Foot on your left.

❹ Continue along the road to a footpath on the left, leading to an abandoned cottage. At the cottage, turn right along a broad track between hedges. Follow the track gently downhill, then up again.

❺ At the belt of trees on your left, look for a wide gate and a stile. Climb the stile and follow the track through the left-hand edge of the trees. When the trees become denser on the left, you begin to descend slightly. At the bottom, bear right along the main track, following the black arrow on a post.

❻ Continue, following two more black arrows close to each other. Another black arrow sends you right at a fork. The track suddenly veers left, away from the power station, and here you turn right at another black arrow. Go over two bridges and a wooden walkway. At the next black arrow, turn left and follow the path to the end of the mound on your right. At the large concrete blocks, turn left along a wide grass track. Follow this path, parallel to the sea, all the way back to the car park at Dunwich.

access information

Take the unclassified road eastwards off the A12, just north-east of Yoxford, signposted to Westleton/Dunwich. In Westleton, turn left along the B1125 signposted Blythburgh/Dunwich, then after 100 m take the turn right signposted Minsmere/Dunwich. Follow signs to Dunwich Heath (right after the track to Mount Pleasant Farm on the right). Park in the National Trust car park.

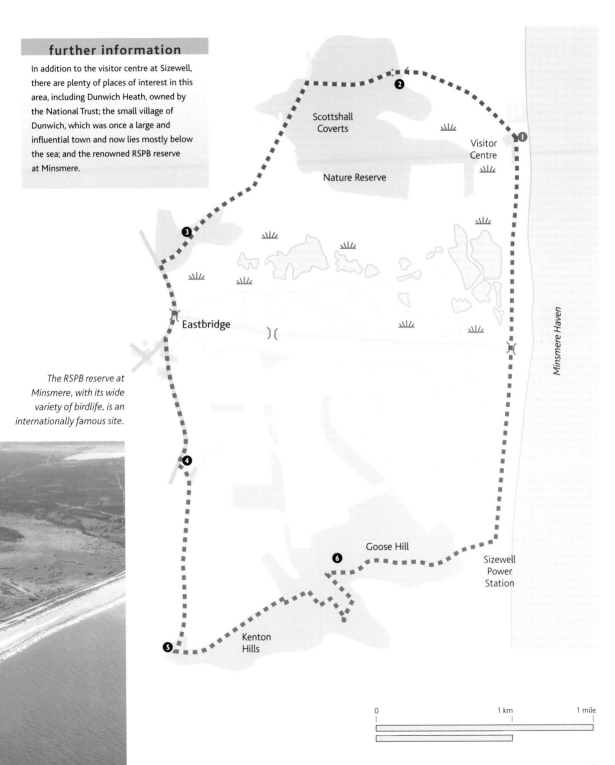

further information

In addition to the visitor centre at Sizewell, there are plenty of places of interest in this area, including Dunwich Heath, owned by the National Trust; the small village of Dunwich, which was once a large and influential town and now lies mostly below the sea; and the renowned RSPB reserve at Minsmere.

Scottshall
Coverts

Nature Reserve

Visitor
Centre

Minsmere Haven

The RSPB reserve at Minsmere, with its wide variety of birdlife, is an internationally famous site.

Eastbridge

Goose Hill

Sizewell
Power
Station

Kenton
Hills

0   1 km   1 mile

▲ Map: Explorer 225

▲ Distance: 9 km/5½ miles

▲ Walk ID: 106 Nicholas Rudd-Jones

Difficulty rating

Time

▲ River, Pub, Mill, National Trust Tea Room, Picnic Site, Nature Reserve, Museum, Good for Kids

St Ives and Hemingford Grey from Hemingford Abbots

This is a charming riverside walk in the Cambridgeshire fens, taking in the delightful villages of Hemingford Abbots and Hemingford Grey as well as the historic town of St Ives. If time permits, there is a working flour mill and a nature reserve in an ancient osier bed to visit en route.

Twelfth-century Hemingford Grey Manor, reputedly one of the oldest continuously inhabited houses in Britain.

❶ From the Axe and Compass pub, take the minor road to the left of the pub. Turn right at the postbox into Meadow Lane. Cross the bridge, then turn right, through the gate and across Hemingford meadow.

❷ Cross the bridge over the lock, then turn left and over the rollers, heading right on the tarmac path. Turn left over a small bridge to Houghton Mill. Follow the Ouse Valley Way footpath sign. Go through the gates and turn right along the gravel path.

❸ Passing the National Trust Tea Room on the right, follow the yellow waymarks across the field, past the caravan site. Carry on until you reach a kissing gate on your left. Go through, then turn right along the gravel path by a brick wall. At the junction, turn left and then right along a minor road.

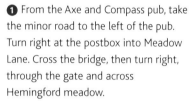

further information

Houghton Mill is open weekends and bank holidays April–September, 2–5.30 p.m. Punts are available for hire at weekends 10 a.m.– 6 p.m. and weekdays during school holidays 2–6 p.m. For info, phone 01480 468184. Holt Island Nature Reserve is open on Sundays April–September 10.30 a.m.– 5 p.m. For info, phone 01480 388442.

4 As the tarmac road swings left, take a small footbridge across the river and follow this road. Pass through St Ives thicket, emerging by the river. At the next junction, go straight ahead (signposted 'Ouse Valley Way'). The path continues through gardens, coming out opposite the church.

5 Go through the churchyard and out via the iron gates. Follow the road to the Jubilee monument and fork right. Turn right at the end of the road and cross the town bridge. Take the first right turn, following the footpath to Hemingford Grey. Go through a gate and cross the meadows on the left-hand path.

6 Go through the gate and join a track. Immediately, take the path to the left to join a road. At the next junction, take the footpath straight ahead. Turn right at the road, then left onto the footpath by the church. Follow the path back to the village. At the road, turn right and return to the Axe and Compass.

Houghton Mill is a major historic attraction along the route of this walk.

access information

Hemingford Abbots is just off the A14 from Huntingdon to Cambridge, between the junctions for Huntingdon and St Ives.

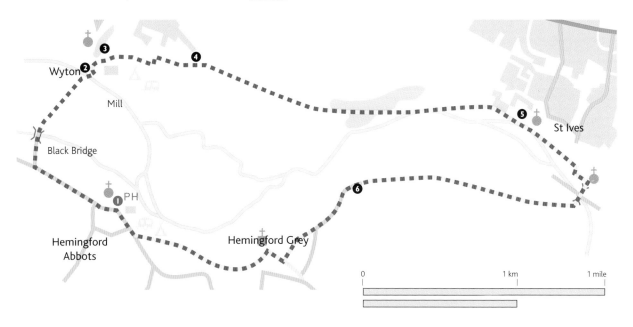

▲ Map: Explorer 207
▲ Distance: 13.69 km/8½ miles
▲ Walk ID: 1301 R. and J. Glynn

Difficulty rating

Time

▲ River, Pub, Church, Wildlife, Birds, Flowers, Great Views, Butterflies, Food Shop

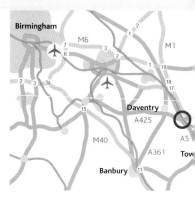

Nether Heyford from Weedon

This diverse walk follows the Nene Way, then the tow-path beside the Grand Union Canal, before following footpaths through fields and meadows to the pretty village of Nether Heyford. The route continues through a beautiful rural landscape, passing Bugbrooke Mill and village before rejoining the canal tow-path.

1 From Weedon Post Office, follow the road to the railway bridge. Past St Peter's churchyard, turn right on the Nene Way. Cross the road and carry on. Fork right off the old Wharf House drive. Cross the canal at bridge 25, go down the steps, then turn left along the tow-path. Turn left at bridge 27 and left along the road.
2 Turn right at the footpath, crossing two fields, then a third, bearing slightly right. Cross a footbridge, a stile and more meadows to a footbridge into a field. Cross a hard track and climb the stile to the right, then cross another field. Climb the stile, and follow the path, turning right by a wall into Nether Heyford.
3 Turn left into Church Lane. Go through the church gate, then turn left. Follow the footpath between trees, then two walls. Cross a narrow road and follow the path opposite. Cross the estate road and carry on. Opposite Brookside Close, turn right.
4 Turn left on the Kislingbury footpath. Cross the river, then go through the kissing gate on the left and follow the field edge. Turn left through another gate, following the field edge to the right. Go through two more gates. Following the hedge line, enter a small copse. Follow the River Nene for a short distance, then take the hard track away.

5 Turn right on the footpath across the fields to Bugbrooke. Climb the stile, follow a narrow path to the road and turn right. At the junction, turn right into Church Lane. Passing the church, turn right towards Weedon, then left on the Old Crown footpath.
6 Turn right at the canal bridge and follow the towpath. Soon after Flore Lane Bridge, climb the stile and follow a track through meadowland. Cross a large field towards a white building. Climb the stile in the corner. Walk up to the road and cross over. Join the Nene Way opposite, and walk along to the canal bridge. Return to the start point.

further information

The walk recalls a time when the Grand Union Canal was an essential route, along which boatmen and their families would travel to and from London with their cargoes. Flour is still produced at Bugbrooke Mill, and in the graveyard of Bugbrooke Church look out for an inscription from Longfellow on a tree.

access information

Weedon lies south of the A5 between Daventry and Northampton. Street parking is available in the village.

The Grand Union Canal, which crosses this route, is a semi-permanent home for houseboat-dwellers.

Weedon

Grand Union Canal

Nether
Heyford

R. Nene

Bugbrooke
Mill

Nene Way

Bugbrooke

0   1 km   1 mile

*This walk takes in a
beautiful English church.*

▲ Map: Explorer 221

▲ Distance: 8.86 km/5½ miles

▲ Walk ID: 992 R. and J. Glynn

Difficulty rating

Time

▲ Pub, Stately Home, Birds, Flowers, Great Views, Butterflies, Food Shop, Woodland

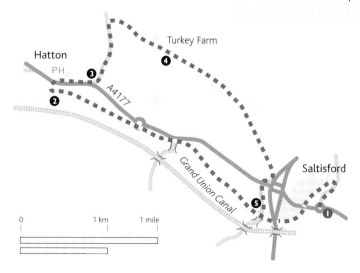

Hatton Locks at Warwick.

Saltisford Basin and Hatton Locks

Much of this walk is on the Grand Union Canal tow-path, following the dramatic climb of the 21 Hatton Locks. The walk then follows a fine bridleway through very pleasant flat farmland, before rejoining the canal to return to Saltisford Basin.

❶ From the car park, turn right, go through the metal gates, then turn left at the end of Budbrooke Road to walk over the canal bridge. Turn left on the footpath opposite the cemetery. After a short distance, veer left off the footpath and go through a gap down onto the canal tow-path. Turn right and walk along the path, passing the first of the 21 Hatton Locks at Hatton Bottom, and then 'Ugly Bridge'.

❷ At bridge 54, the route leaves the canal. Walk with the large white house on your right, and go through the kissing gate in the corner, beneath a tree. Walk uphill to pass the Waterman pub, turning right beside it. Turn right onto the pavement along the road, then cross the road to take the left fork to Beausale.

❸ After a short distance, turn left onto a minor road, which gradually climbs to reach Ashwood Lodge. Turn right on a bridleway towards Turkey Farm House. Go through the metal gate beside the farmhouse and carry on, passing a pond. Turn right at a marker and walk around the field edge.

❹ Go through a gap on the left, beside an oak tree, and follow the edge of the field on a permissive path to the far corner, turning right into the next field. Walk on with Blackbrake Plantation on the left and a wooded area on the right, still following the field edges, which zigzag before Wedgnock Farm. Pass the farm on a track to the right and follow the track to the road. Cross by the traffic lights, and walk along Budbrooke Road ahead, passing the Fire Safety Headquarters before reaching the canal bridge.

❺ Turn right over the road and then go down onto the canal footpath and turn left. Retrace your steps to the Saltisford Basin car park.

further information

The 21 Hatton Locks are a spectacular sight, with their tall, white-topped paddles, white-tipped gates and white edging around the lock entrances. Once a hub of working narrow boats, the locks are now used only by leisure craft, and the sight of a loaded pair of boats, crewed by the boatman and his family, has gone for ever.

access information

From the A452 between Warwick and Birmingham, follow the sign to Canal Centre, Saltisford, and turn left into the centre car park.

▲ Map: Explorer 222

▲ Distance: 9.66 km/6 miles

▲ Walk ID: 1481 R. and J. Glynn

Difficulty rating

Time

▲ Lake, Pub, Church, Wildlife, Birds, Flowers, Great Views, Butterflies, Food Shop

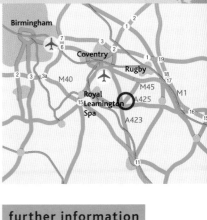

Calcutt Locks from Stockton

This great little walk can almost be entitled 'a marina walk', as it visits three – Ventnor Farm Marina and Calcutt Marina, both on the Grand Union Canal, and Napton Marina, on the North Oxford Canal.

❶ Following the Napton road, cross the sports field to a gap in the far corner. Follow the field edge to the stile. Turn left on the road. At the metal gate, turn right and cross a field diagonally left, then a large meadow, following the hedge. Cross another meadow, then climb two stiles through pasture, heading for the top left corner.

❷ Turn left on a track, then right at the road. Turn left through the gate opposite Hill Cottage onto a bridleway. Go through another gate and follow the path. Turn left over Tomlow Bridge, left onto the tow-path, and left again under the bridge to walk beside the Grand Union Canal.

❸ At Calcutt Locks, walk to the top of the flight. Cross the top lock gate, then a footbridge by the shop, turning left by the railings. Turn right over the footbridge, then left. Turn right through an opening between the two sections of reservoir. Crossing a wooden bridge, turn left.

❹ Turn right through a signed gap in the fence and cross the meadow to a gap in the hedge. Cross another meadow. Enter another field, aiming for a stile at the top. Walk over to a metal gate and on to the North Oxford Canal tow-path. Turn right under the bridge and walk to bridge 111. Turn right through a gate to the road.

❺ Turn immediately right through a gate and cross two fields. Cross a stile, a footbridge, and three more fields. Climb the stile and follow the edge of two more fields. When the hedge turns away, walk on, cross a stile and a footbridge, and head towards the sewage works. Cross the next field to the stile in the corner. Turn left onto a track, then right on a private road. Follow the road back into Stockton.

Taking a narrowboat down the Grand Union Canal.

further information

The paths across the fields and meadows are well-defined and easy to follow. The Napton Reservoir is surrounded by natural meadowland, where wonderful wild flowers grow. There is also a huge reed bed near the point at which you head away from the reservoir. As you walk, look out for the Napton Windmill – it comes into view near the start of the route, and again at the reservoir.

access information

From the A423 Banbury to Coventry road, take the A426 towards Rugby, and turn off on an unclassified road to the village of Stockton.

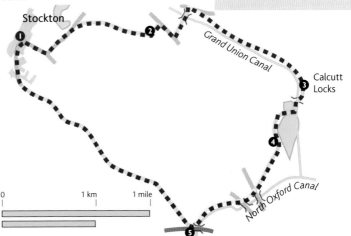

The woodland and hillside walks of Central England reveal Herefordshire hills, the Peak District and the Lincolnshire Wolds. Highlights include Barnack Hills and Holes, Long Melford and Gradbach Wood.

Difficulty rating

Time

▲ Lake, Pub, Toilets, Museum, Church, Stately Home, Gift Shop, Food Shop, Good for Kids, Public Transport, Restaurant, Woodland

Woodland in Melbourne Parks.

Melbourne Parks

This simple countryside walk begins and ends in the ancient village of Melbourne. The parish church is one of the finest surviving examples of Norman ecclesiastical architecture in the country, and dates from the mid-12th century.

1 Starting at the junction into Melbourne Hall and park, follow Blackwell Lane out of Melbourne. Just before the road bends to the right, there is a footpath sign on the right. Follow the footpath into the fields. Almost immediately bear half left to a stile and follow the path diagonally across the fields. The next stile is under the trees. Continue across the fields to the main track from the park.

2 Cross the cattle grid and then a stile, just off to the left. Follow the path diagonally across two fields up the hill towards a big tree and a farmhouse on the horizon. Leave the fields and go through a gap in the trees ahead of you. Follow the path through the next field, going down to join Green Lane.

3 Turn right and follow the lane until it bends sharply right. Branch left to follow the bridleway. Cross a small stream and carry on. Turn right where the path splits, and head up the hill towards the trees. Follow the path through the woods and come out in a small field.

4 Cross the field to another plantation of trees, called Paddock Pool. Cross a small bridge over a stream and come out of the woods into another field. Cross the field to its far diagonal corner. Turn right and cross the stile. The path continues along a grassy lane.

5 As the lane bends left to the farmhouse, keep right and aim for the trees ahead. Climb a few steps to a stile, then continue on the right-hand edge of the next field. Follow the footpath signs through the fields.

6 Leaving the last field, join the metalled track through Melbourne Park. Turn left and walk towards the Melbourne Pool. Following this track, return to the start of the walk.

access information

Melbourne is off the A514 south of Derby. Pass through Stanton-by-Bridge and take the B587 towards Melbourne. In Melbourne, follow signs for Melbourne Hall. There is limited parking outside the church.

further information

Melbourne is the second largest town in South Derbyshire, with a population of around 5,000. This ancient town is in the centre of a fertile market-gardening area.

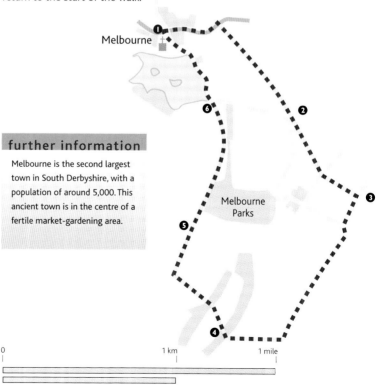

▲ Map: Explorer 234

▲ Distance: 6 km/3¾ miles

▲ Walk ID: 32 Nicholas Rudd-Jones

Difficulty rating

Time

▲ Pub, Church, Wildlife, Birds, Flowers

Barnack Hills and Holes

This simple stroll starts at the enchanting and aptly named Barnack Hills and Holes, where ragstone was quarried to build Peterborough Cathedral in the 12th century – you will see a few lumps in the road at Southorpe village.

❶ Choose one of the many paths across the nature reserve and head for the south-west edge. Go through a wooden gate alongside the big stone wall of Walcot Hall.

❷ Follow the path between the wall and a field. At the end of the wall, where the path meets the road, turn left onto a gravelled track marked 'Public Bridleway', passing Walcot Hall on your left. At the next corner of the park wall, continue ahead on another gravelled track.

❸ When the track veers left, keep straight on to the right of a low stone wall ahead of you and take the path along the field edge. Pass through a wooden gate and follow the field edge, heading for a metal gate to the right of two oak trees.

❹ Go through the gate and head for the road, keeping the wall on your right. Turn left onto the road to Southorpe. Where the road starts to veer right at the end of the village, by Hall Farm, climb a stile into a field. Head for a gate and another stile at the far side of the field, then aim for a small group of cottages.

❺ At the cottages, cross the road and go through a wooden gate into fields. Walk towards the left-hand corner of the thin hedge ahead of you. Keep the hedge on your right and follow the path into Barnack village, past the bowling green and cricket ground on your left,

alongside a stone wall, and then between trees. At the road, turn left. Follow the road round to the right at the Fox and Hounds pub and take the next left. Shortly afterwards, turn left again, passing the Millstone pub on the way back to the car.

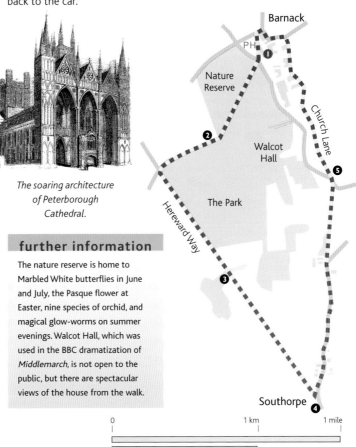

The soaring architecture of Peterborough Cathedral.

access information

Barnack is south of the A16 from Stamford to Market Deeping. Park in a little lay-by at the main entrance to the nature reserve.

further information

The nature reserve is home to Marbled White butterflies in June and July, the Pasque flower at Easter, nine species of orchid, and magical glow-worms on summer evenings. Walcot Hall, which was used in the BBC dramatization of *Middlemarch*, is not open to the public, but there are spectacular views of the house from the walk.

0   1 km   1 mile

▲ Map: Explorer 234
▲ Distance: 8 km/5 miles
▲ Walk ID: 9 Nicholas Rudd-Jones

Difficulty rating

Time

▲ River, Pub, Toilets, Museum, Church, Wildlife, Birds, Flowers, Great Views

Easton on the Hill from Stamford

This splendid walk begins in Stamford Meadows and carries on to give fine views of the Welland Valley. The route passes through Easton, a typical Welland Valley village, and returns to Stamford through glorious countryside and woodland.

❶ From the car park, cross a bridge across a tributary and cross the meadow to a gate. Go through and follow the path across the meadow. Pass the stone seat with a plaque commemorating Queen Boudicca, and follow the river to the Broadeng Bridge. Cross over and continue to follow the river.

❷ Follow a marked path slightly to the left and go through the tunnel under the A1. Cross a bridge and a field, and climb the wooden steps up and over the railway crossing. On the other side, walk through an overgrown stretch into a long field. Follow the path leading up towards the Easton slope.

❸ At the corner of the field, go through a gap in the hedge and cross the field to a stile. Climb this stile and the next one and carry on to Easton, coming out in Church Street. Turn left at the church into the village. After the War Memorial, turn left to the A43 and turn left again for a short distance. Cross carefully to a signed footpath.

❹ Follow this track, passing first between two fields and then through the woods. With the Wothorpe ruins on your right, walk down a stone track then climb a stile to a footpath on your right. Walk down towards the A1.

❺ Go through the tunnel under the A1 and immediately turn right, following the field edge to the next field. Turn left towards Stamford. Climb a stile, cross the field and climb another stile.

❻ Follow the path between houses then walk along an entrance road. The path continues between two hedges to the left of a Victorian house. At the next field, cross diagonally left to a bridge over a stream. Cross another field to the main road. Cross straight over and walk back to the meadows.

The resident deer at Stamford's Burghley Park are just a small part of the wildlife interest in this area.

further information

There are many types of butterflies to be seen in the woods on this walk, particularly Peacocks, Red Admirals, Small Tortoiseshells and Speckled Woods. A good time to see butterflies is late September when the ivy comes into flower, a valuable source of nectar for the long winter months ahead.

access information

Parking is available in the car park at Stamford Meadows.

There is a regular train service to Stamford station – the start of the walk is two minutes from the station. Go to www.railtrack.co.uk for information on train times.

The Peacock (far left) and the Red Admiral (left) are just two of the many types of butterfly that can be found in the woods along this walk.

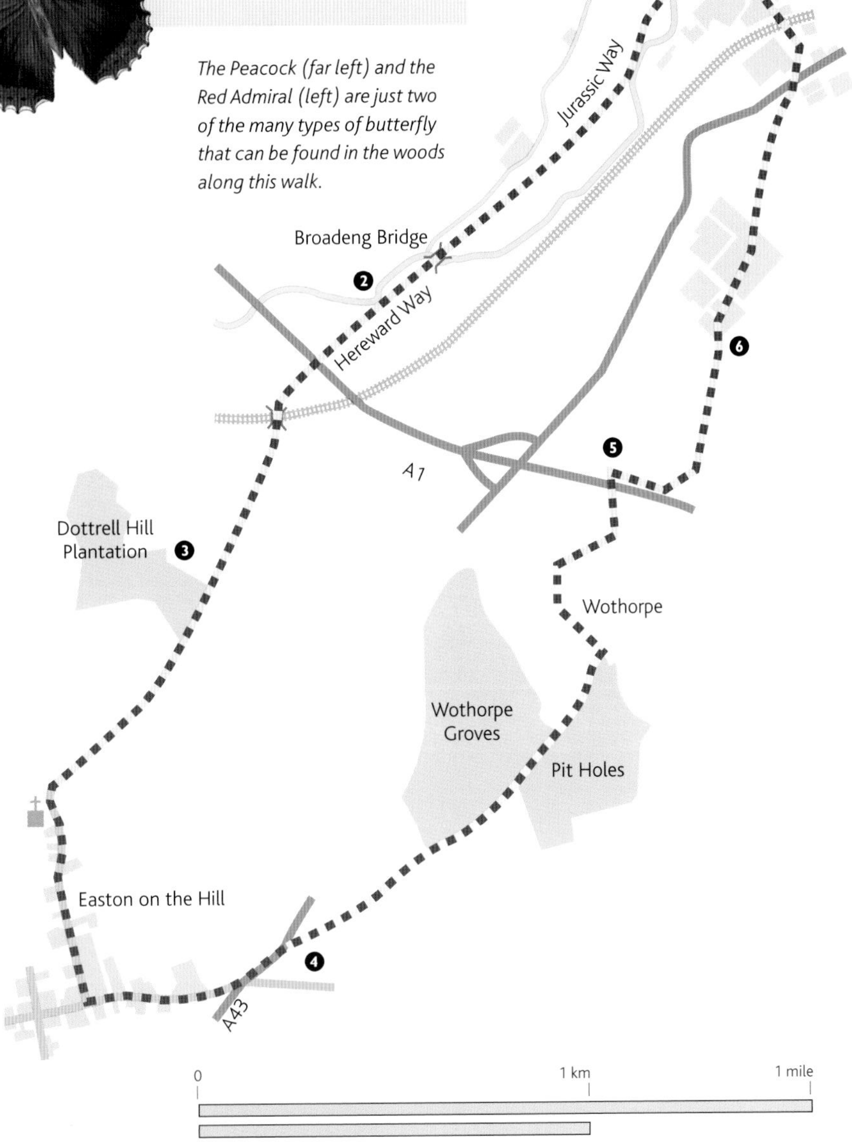

Stamford

Jurassic Way

Broadeng Bridge

Hereward Way

A1

Dottrell Hill Plantation

Wothorpe

Wothorpe Groves

Pit Holes

Easton on the Hill

A43

0   1 km   1 mile

▲ Map: Explorer 273
▲ Distance: 13.69 km/8½ miles
▲ Walk ID: 473 E. Hutchinson

Difficulty rating

Time

▲ Hills, Pub, Churches, Wildlife, Birds, Flowers, Great Views

Tetford and Worlaby from Maidenwell

This walk in the Lincolnshire Wolds descends to Farforth and follows a wonderful deserted valley to Oxcombe. From Tetford there is a steep climb, skirting Worlaby to Ruckland. If time permits, visit the churches at Oxcombe, Tetford and Ruckland.

❶ From the starting point, go through the gate and walk diagonally left across the field towards some trees. The path joins a track which leads to a metal footpath sign. Turn right, keeping the hedge on your left. Follow the path, descending first to pass a wood then following the valley to Oxcombe. If you wish, make a detour to the church.

❷ Turn right and walk along the lane to the first waymark on the left. Cross a small paddock to another lane and turn left. At the next junction, turn right towards Belchford, then turn left on the bridleway towards Glebe Farm Low Yard. After a short distance turn left at another waymark and follow the bridleway to Tetford.

❸ At Tetford, go straight ahead and bear left at the first junction. Visit the church if you like, then follow the lane to the left of the church. At the end go through the cottage entrance. Cross a stile left of the greenhouse. Follow the path across a small paddock, over a stile and up and over the hill. Follow the path through a paddock.

❹ Climb another stile and turn left on the track, then diagonally right across the field. Turn right and cross the road. Beside the gate to Worlaby Farm, cross the stile, the paddock and another stile to follow the well-waymarked farm road through the estate grounds.

❺ At the end of the estate road, turn right. Detour to Ruckland Church if you wish. The walk route turns left at the top of a bank. Follow the path, which is clearly waymarked all the way to Farforth. At Farforth, turn right onto the lane and then left by some fencing. Follow the track ahead to rejoin the track you started out on.

access information

Farforth lies west of the A16 Louth to Skegness road. A wide verge provides good parking for an unlimited number of cars.

The typical orange-red earth of the Lincolnshire Wolds, with the town of Louth in the background.

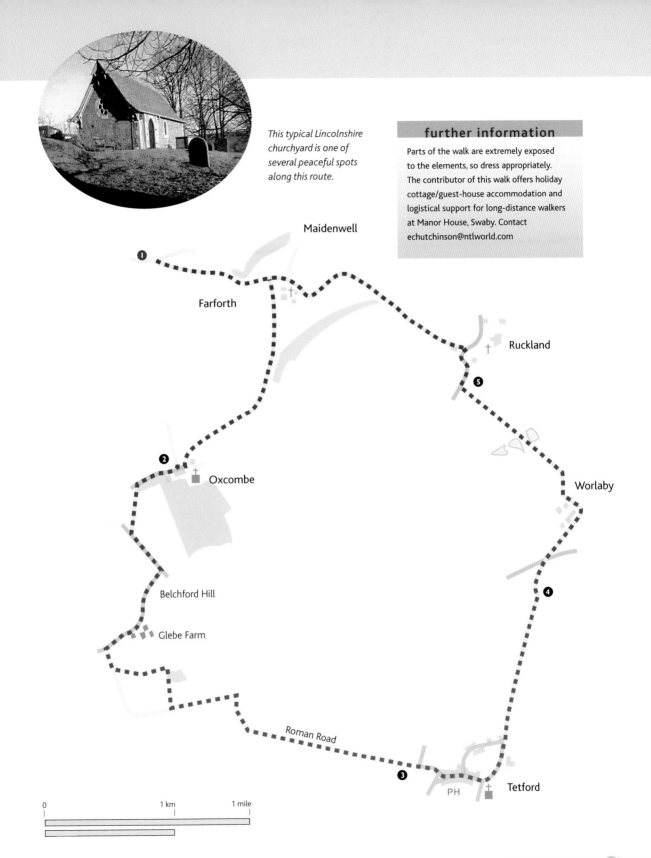

This typical Lincolnshire churchyard is one of several peaceful spots along this route.

further information

Parts of the walk are extremely exposed to the elements, so dress appropriately. The contributor of this walk offers holiday cottage/guest-house accommodation and logistical support for long-distance walkers at Manor House, Swaby. Contact echutchinson@ntlworld.com

Maidenwell

Farforth

Ruckland

❶

❺

❷ Oxcombe

Worlaby

Belchford Hill

❹

Glebe Farm

Roman Road

❸

Tetford

PH

0   1 km   1 mile

Difficulty rating

Time

▲ River, Pub, Toilets, Church, Stately Home, National Trust/NTS, Wildlife, Birds, Flowers, Great Views, Restaurant, Tea Shop, Woodland, Ancient Monument

The Stour Valley Way and Glemsford from Long Melford

This walk begins in Long Melford, an idyllic Suffolk village surrounded by sweeping parkland and rolling countryside. There are several great manor houses, including the Tudor Long Melford Hall and the moated Kentwell Hall.

1 From the car park, turn left. Cross the A1092 to the church. Turn left in the churchyard, go through a gateway, then cross a stile. Turn right across another stile and a paddock. Cross two more stiles, passing woodland to a third stile. Walk across to another stile and turn towards Kentwell Hall. Just before the gates, turn left. Go through two gates, then bear right. Follow the track, passing fields then woodland.

2 Turn left. Follow the path, with woodland then a ditch and field on your left. When you reach trees ahead and a gap on the left, turn right. Where the track goes left to a farm, carry on and cross a footbridge. Follow the track to the road. Turn right, then left at Mill Farmhouse.

3 Cross a metal footbridge then turn half right to a bridge over a ditch. Turn right with the ditch on your right. At the end of the field on your left, turn left and walk on to meet Park Lane. Turn left, then turn right along the left side of a field. At the end, turn left along a signposted footpath.

further information

At Kentwell Hall, there are frequent reconstructions of life as it would have been when the house was built in 1564. Authentic clothing is worn, and there are demonstrations of cooking, weaving and spinning in Tudor style.

access information

Long Melford lies slightly north of Sudbury and just west of the A134 from Sudbury to Bury St Edmunds. The walk starts from the free car park opposite Melford Hall, and there is plenty of additional parking.

This view of the village of Nayland, in the Stour Valley, has remained unchanged for centuries.

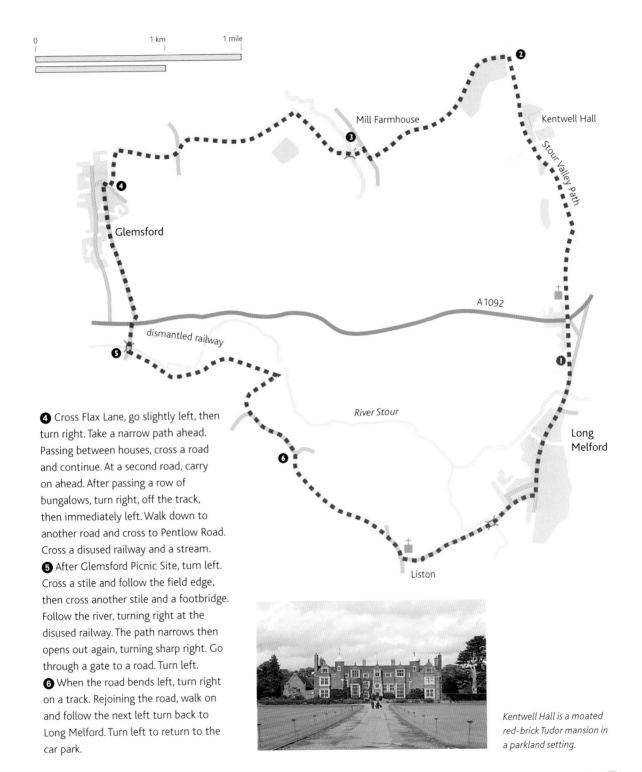

Mill Farmhouse

Kentwell Hall

Stour Valley Path

Glemsford

A 1092

dismantled railway

River Stour

Long Melford

Liston

4 Cross Flax Lane, go slightly left, then turn right. Take a narrow path ahead. Passing between houses, cross a road and continue. At a second road, carry on ahead. After passing a row of bungalows, turn right, off the track, then immediately left. Walk down to another road and cross to Pentlow Road. Cross a disused railway and a stream.

5 After Glemsford Picnic Site, turn left. Cross a stile and follow the field edge, then cross another stile and a footbridge. Follow the river, turning right at the disused railway. The path narrows then opens out again, turning sharp right. Go through a gate to a road. Turn left.

6 When the road bends left, turn right on a track. Rejoining the road, walk on and follow the next left turn back to Long Melford. Turn left to return to the car park.

Kentwell Hall is a moated red-brick Tudor mansion in a parkland setting.

▲ Map: Explorer OL 24

▲ Distance: 11 km/6¾ miles

▲ Walk ID: 1041 Barry Smith

Difficulty rating

Time

▲ Hills or Fells, River, Wildlife, Great Views, Moor, Woodland

Stockport

Macclesfield

A537

Buxton

A54

A53

A6

A523

Leek

Stoke-on-Trent

Gradbach Wood and The Roaches from Gradbach

This is a magnificent walk with plenty of contrast. From Gradbach, you follow the beautiful River Dane and Black Brook, followed by forest paths in deep woodland, before climbing to The Roaches, a rocky moorland ridge.

❶ Turn right out of the car park and fork right to the Youth Hostel. Follow a short lane on the left of the Hostel car park to the corner. Go up the steps and path and climb the stile. The path widens into a farm track. Climb the stile in the wall ahead and turn right downhill to Castors Bridge. Cross the footbridge into Forest Bottom, and follow the sign left.

❷ Continue up the path beside Black Brook and through Gradbach Wood. At the next fork in the path, take the lower one to continue beside, but above, Black Brook. Join a wider path coming from the right, and continue left.

❸ At the top of a hill, take the sign for Roach End over a small stream. Follow the path, mostly uphill, into open countryside. Cross a stile, then another squeeze stile almost immediately on the left leading to a road.

❹ Cross the road and follow the path opposite, uphill and by a wall, onto The Roaches. Climb to the trig point and carry on. At the deep cleft in the ridge on your right, follow a path going down to the next left turn. Follow the path along the base of the cliff to the end.

❺ Ignore the steps to the right and take the path downhill into the col, towards the gate and path leading to Hen Cloud.

Ascend Hen Cloud if you wish. If not, turn left and follow the main path straight ahead. After a farm track, you reach a minor road.

❻ Follow the road to the right, then turn left opposite Newstone Farm. At the next junction, bear left, then follow the green lane signposted to Gradbach across the fields. Turn right, passing the fork to the Youth Hostel, and return to the car park.

access information

From Buxton, take the A53 Leek road for about 8 km. At the sign for Flash, turn right on a minor road, bearing left for Gradbach after 0.5 km. In another 3.5 km. turn left, signed for Gradbach Youth Hostel, then turn right into the car park.

The spectacular view from The Roaches is well worth the climb.

further information

This area is rich in myths and legends. There are stories of a headless rider and a tall man dressed in green, which could be folk recollections of the story of Sir Gawain in Arthurian legend. Lud's Church, a cave on The Roaches estate, is said to be the legendary Green Chapel in a 14th-century poem reciting Sir Gawain's story.

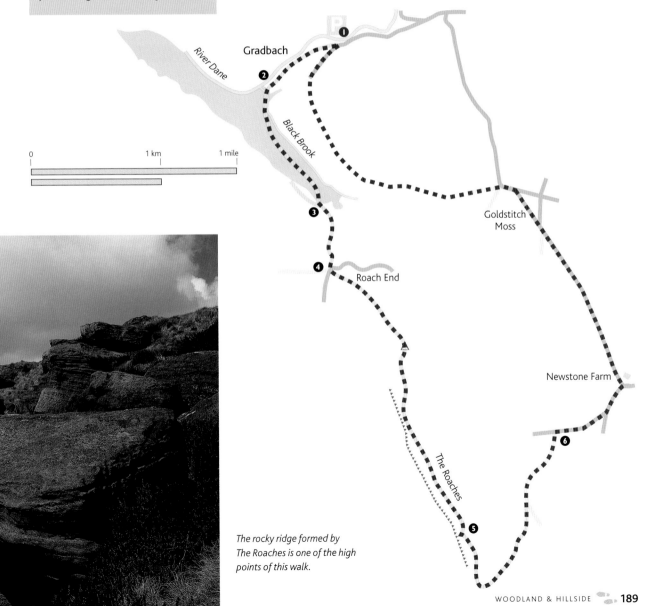

The rocky ridge formed by The Roaches is one of the high points of this walk.

Index

acknowledgements

The publishers wish to thank the following for the use of pictures: TONY BROTHERTON: p.15. CAMERON COLLECTION: p.149. COLLECTIONS: pp.14 Dennis Barnes, 145 Jill Swainson, 150 Robert Deane, 160 Philip Craven, 162 Robert Pilgrim, 188/9 + 189 Robin Weaver. CORBIS: pp.56 Ric Ergenbright, 18 Roger Tidman, 22 Ric Ergenbright, 44 Michael Busselle, 45 Julie Meech/Ecoscene, Sandro Vannini, 48/9 Ric Ergenbright, 52 Michael Busselle, 53 Peter Hulme/Ecoscene, 57 Michael Boys, 58 Peter M Wilson, 92 John Heseltine, 93 Eye Ubiquitous, 94 John Heseltine, 66 Richard Klune, 70 Jon Sparks, 72 Andrew Brown/Ecoscene, 74/5 Patrick Ward, 104 John Heseltine, 106 Alan Towse/Ecoscene, 78/9 Michael Busselle, 80 Wildcountry, 87 Michael Busselle, 118 Roy Westlake, 120 Jason Hawkes, 121 Bob Krist, 122/3 Michael Boys, 125 Bob Krist, 124 Adam Woolfitt, 126 Michael Busselle, 127 John Farmer, 110/11 Chinch Gryniewicz, 113 Peter Hulme, 132 Michael Busselle, 134 Robert Estall, 137 Bob Krist, 143 Adam Woolfitt, 148 Adam Woolfitt, 156 John Farmar/Cordaiy Photo Library Ltd., 154 Yann Arthus-Bertrand, 169 Roger Tidman, 170/1 David Hoskins, 172 Michael Boys, 173 John Heseltine, 174/5 Greenhalf Photography, 176 Buddy Mays, 177 Colin Garratt/Milepost, 182 + 183 Michael S Yamashita, 186 Robert Estall. GETTY IMAGES: pp.16 Graeme Norways/Stone, 26 Chris Close/The Image Bank, 28 David Paterson/Stone, 40/1 Chris Close/The Image Bank, 41 Trevor Wood/Stone, 60/1 Colin Raw/Stone, 66 Walter Bibikov, 130 Chris Simpson/Stone. RON AND JENNY GLYNN: p.175. DAN GRANT: pp.20, 23. JIM GRINDLE: pp.69, 155T, 86. HUTCHISON PICTURE LIBRARY: pp. 96/7 Bernard Gerard, 136, 159, 185. JEAN HARDMAN: pp.59, 60. JOYCE AND DOUG HOWAT: p.84. JUDE HOWAT: pp. 22, 32, 42, 43, 54, 55. STEWART HOWAT: p. 180. STEPHANIE KEDIK: p. 168. ALAN KINGSLAND: p.135. OLIVER O'BRIEN: pp. 30, 31. MICHAEL PARKIN: p. 56. PAT ROBERTS: pp. 100, 211. PETER SALENIEKS: pp.101, 108, 109. BRIAN & ANNE SANDLAND: p.187. COLIN AND JOANNE SIMPSON: pp. 34, 35. MIKE TAYLOR: p.35. JOHN THORN: pp. 98, 99, 112. DAVID L.WHITE p. 157.